Neurotic Styles

Neurotic Styles

DAVID SHAPIRO

Foreword by ROBERT P. KNIGHT

The Austen Riggs Center Monograph Series Number 5

Basic Books, Inc., *Publishers*

NEW YORK • LONDON

Library of Congress Catalog Card Number 65-23044
SBN: 465-09502-X
Printed in the United States of America
Designed by Sophie Adler

20 19 18 17 16 15 14 13 12 11

To Gerry

Foreword

David Shapiro began developing his ideas about neurotic styles, beginning with the obsessive-compulsive style, in the last several years of his association with the Austen Riggs Center. He presented an early draft of a paper on this topic at a Riggs seminar in January 1960. The present Chapter 2 is a far cry from that early draft presentation, but it is clear that the gestation of the book began at that time and with the encouragement provided by the Riggs staff at the seminar. I believe that it was I who suggested that he do a series of papers on various styles from the same point of view, for I thought that he had an important contribution to make to psychoanalytic ego psychology, particularly to the psychology of character formation. Dr. Shapiro did, indeed, continue with his studies of style, and this book is the result.

Inasmuch as the book was conceived at the Austen Riggs Center, I am very happy to have it come out as Austen Riggs Center Monograph Number 5, even though the author left Riggs to return to private practice in Los Angeles five years ago. I have learned much from the conceptualization and descriptions of character styles that Dr. Shapiro has worked out in such a scholarly manner, and I venture to predict that his book will come to be widely regarded as an outstanding contribution to psychoanalytic ego psychology and characterology.

ROBERT P. KNIGHT, M.D.

Stockbridge, Massachusetts
July 1965

Acknowledgments

This book was planned and its writing begun while I was still a member of the staff of the Austen Riggs Center at Stockbridge, Massachusetts. I owe much to many people there. In particular, I want to express my gratitude to Dr. Robert P. Knight, Medical Director of Riggs, and Dr. Joseph O. Chassell, Senior Staff Member, who consistently encouraged this project and read the entire manuscript with a careful and critical attention from which the book has profited very much. I have been helped, also, by many suggestions from others who have read portions of the manuscript or heard those parts of it I have presented at Riggs seminars on three occasions and by those colleagues and friends with whom I have discussed many of these points and issues over the years. I would like to mention especially Drs. Jean Schimek, now of Albert Einstein Medical Center in Philadelphia; Robert A. Harris, the present Chief Psychologist at Riggs; Richard Rouse, of Williams College; and Veikko Tähka, now of Helsinki.

I would also like to express my appreciation of others who taught and influenced me in many ways while I was at the Riggs Center, particularly the late Dr. David Rapaport, Prof. Erik H. Erikson, and Dr. Roy Schafer. Finally, I want to acknowledge my debt to the late Dr. Hellmuth Kaiser, whose psychological understanding has influenced me significantly.

Finally, let me use this chance to express my appreciation to Mrs. Betty Homich of Stockbridge and Mrs. JoAnn Smith of Los Angeles for their competent and patient secretarial work on the manuscript.

Some of the material of Chapter 2 appeared originally in my article "Aspects of Obsessive-Compulsive Style," *Psychiatry,* XXV, No. 1 (1962).

DAVID SHAPIRO

Los Angeles, California
July 1965

Contents

Neurotic Styles

Introduction

This book had its beginnings in the noticing of certain facts about various pathological conditions and certain specific clinical conclusions—long before I would have considered these to represent a "point of view." There is a point of view, I realized later, but I did not write this book so much to expound that point of view as to apply it. It is, therefore, a clinical book on neurosis or neurotic functioning, and, if I take some pains in this introduction to explain its orientation, it is not with an interest in theoretical argument, but to guide the reader in his understanding of the clinical chapters that follow. In the last chapter, I shall consider some more general, theoretical implications of the point of view.

Let me explain what I mean by "neurotic styles." By "style," I mean a form or mode of functioning—the way or manner of a given area of behavior—that is identifiable, in an individual, through a range of his specific acts. By "neurotic styles," I mean those modes of functioning that seem characteristic, respectively, of the various neurotic conditions. I shall consider here, particularly, ways of thinking and perceiving, ways of experiencing emotion, modes of subjective experience in general, and modes of activity that are associated with various pathologies. It is not my aim to be exhaustive nor even systematic, and it is clear that there are many interesting aspects of style that cannot even be touched on here—for example, body-movement styles. But I hope to provide at least an outline of four major neurotic styles: obsessive-compulsive, paranoid, hysterical, and impulsive.

A manner or style of functioning is not always easy to identify. We are usually inclined to pay attention to the content of a communication or an act, and noticing its manner requires a different, perhaps in some respects more passive sort of attention. Yet, when one does notice the manner, it is often a striking and vivid experience, a new aspect of a familiar thing.

I first became interested in the forms or styles of functioning —particularly of thinking and perceiving—characteristic of various sorts of psychopathology through working with psychological tests. In tests, particularly in the Rorschach test, ways of thinking and perceiving are (or, at least, should be) the primary material from which inferences concerning diagnosis, defense mechanisms, and character traits are drawn. It seemed to me that these ways of thinking—ordinarily used to identify defense mechanisms, traits, and diagnostic syndromes and, in general, to draw a picture of psychological makeup—must in themselves represent psychological structures of importance, and these structures might be of a more general type than the specific traits or mechanisms that could be inferred from them. If, for example, it is possible to identify certain defense mechanisms and specific symptomatic characteristics of an obsessional kind in a given style of thinking and perception, that style can be conceived of as representing a psychological structure in its own right. If, as is often the case, minor variations of the same style of thinking suggest other, sometimes adaptive features and traits as well, then perhaps this general style of thinking may be considered a matrix from which the various traits, symptoms, and defense mechanisms crystallize. It seemed plausible, in other words, that mode of thinking might be one factor that determines the *shape* or *form* of symptom, defense mechanism, and adaptive trait as well.

These questions are raised with particular clarity in connection with the results and procedures of psychological tests, because tests are designed for or, at least, are often well suited to bringing formal qualities of thinking and perception to light. But the questions themselves are general ones. Is it possible to describe forms of functioning—ways of thinking, experiencing, and behaving—that are characteristic of the various sorts of pathology, styles of functioning that comprise a matrix for specific symptoms and traits and that determine the shape that a given symptom or trait may take in a given individual?

The simple fact of human consistency over broad areas of functioning argues for such a concept, but this fact has a more specific clinical manifestation. Every reader with clinical experience and, for that matter, every sensitive person will know that symptoms or outstanding pathological traits regularly appear in contexts of attitudes, interests, intellectual inclinations and endowments, and even vocational aptitudes and social affinities with which the given symptom or trait seems to have a certain consistency. We are not surprised, for instance, to hear that a bookkeeper or a scholar has developed an obsessional type of neurosis or that a woman who comes to psychotherapy because of severe emotional outbursts is an actress who is a bright and vivid social companion but is uninterested in and rather uninformed about science or mathematics. One feels, in such cases, that the nature of the symptom fits the nature of the activities, inclinations, and disinclinations that make up its background. Or, to mention a different type of example, if we hear that a patient in an acutely paranoid state, with intricate and "systematized" delusions, was, before the onset of his present condition, a severely obsessional person or a rigid and dogmatic compulsive, again we would very likely be aware of some consistency or similarity between the two conditions, although we might not be able to explain that similarity with great clarity.

These consistencies in an individual's functioning do not seem to be explainable as manifestations of specific defense mechanisms or derivatives of specific drive contents; they are too broad and extensive for that. They are formal consistencies; I would venture to say that they are consistencies of individual style. I do not mean to say that any single mode or style can describe all areas of an individual's functioning, but only that styles or modes may be found that are capable of describing general aspects of function (such as cognition, emotional experience, and the like), modes that themselves will then be related and organized. Such consistencies of individual functioning as those between symptom and adaptive trait may be conceived of as reflecting such general modes, giving shape alike to symptom and nonsymptom, to defense against impulse and adaptive expression of impulse. They are, presumably, slow to change and, therefore, guarantee not only an individual's consistency, but also his relative stability over long periods of time.[1] Still, it must be admitted that these consistencies only have the status of clinical impressions until such forms of functioning that may explain them actually can be described.

This view of general forms or styles of functioning as a matrix for specific traits or symptoms touches on two problems that have figured significantly in psychoanalysis but have never been resolved satisfactorily. The first is the problem of the "choice of neurosis," that is, the problem of what factors dispose a given person to develop symptoms of a particular form; the second is the problem of understanding character. These two problems are, in certain ways, intimately related; in fact, they may easily be considered as different aspects of the same essential problem. That is to say, the disposition to one or another

---

[1] This is illustrated in the following observation by Escalona and Heider, referring to their developmental study: "As one notes behavioral alterations from infancy to—in the case of our study—later preschool ages, one knows that not a single behavior has remained the same, yet one is struck with the inherent continuity of behavioral style and of the child's pattern of adaptation" (Sibylle K. Escalona and Grace Heider, *Prediction and Outcome* [New York: Basic Books, 1959], p. 9).

specific form of symptom may be regarded as essentially a problem of character, and, further, character may be regarded as consisting of the configuration in an individual of just such general and relatively stable forms of functioning as we have been discussing. But these problems were seen differently in the early days of psychoanalysis.

As has often been pointed out, the main interest of psychoanalysis in its early development was the study of instinctual drives and their vicissitudes. Accordingly, the pathological symptom was studied chiefly in this aspect. The content of the specific symptom and not the general form of functioning was studied, and the problem of the choice of neurosis was one of identification of the drive content represented in the symptom and correlation of it with a developmental (psychosexual) phase. Beyond this, the question remained of establishing the reasons for the specific psychosexual fixation.

What are the limitations of this understanding? Whereas some aspects of the neurotic symptom may be understood in this way, other aspects are not clearly traceable to the content of the original drive or the earlier drive conflict. Thus, whereas it is possible to see reaction-formation against anal-erotic impulses in the compulsive's hand-washing or overconcern with cleanliness, the reliance on reaction-formation itself (in contrast, for example, with reliance on the mechanism of repression), the moralistic attitudes, and the intensity of activity and work that are usually associated with such symptoms are not easily derived from the specific content of the drive conflict. Freud was aware of the insufficiency of an attempt to solve the problem of symptom choice exclusively on the basis of libidinal development, conflict, and fixation. He wrote:

We know that a full understanding of any neurotic predisposition from the developmental point of view is never complete without taking into account not merely the stage of libido-development at which fixation occurs but also the stage of ego-development. Our concern has been confined to libido-development, however, and consequently does not afford all the information we are entitled to expect. At the present time little is known. . . .[2]

There was as yet no theory of generalized characteristic forms of functioning nor of "character" in that sense. The interest of the early psychoanalytic papers on character[3] was, rather, an interest in discovering representations or derivatives of instinctual contents (either continuations of early drives, sublimations of them, or reaction-formations against them) within specific traits or clusters of traits.

It is true that there is, in those papers of Freud, Jones, and Abraham, some suggestion of the persistence of relatively general forms of behavior and experience not always clearly tied to symbolic representations of their original objects and sometimes possessing considerable adaptive power—in other words, of the generalization of an instinctual mode into a broad style of functioning; but these are only suggestions or incidental ideas and it is obvious that the main point and the excitement of discovery is elsewhere. The concept of sublimation, particularly, often suggests an idea of the generalization of an instinctual mode beyond its original object, but this suggestion is most likely contributed by a contemporary reading, the concept's actual meaning being, rather, the substitution of alternate routes to the original drive object or a representation of it. In other words, concepts of certain ego forms, tendencies, or mechanisms (for example, sublimation and reaction-formation) are to be found in these papers, but they are not their main point and they do

---

[2] Sigmund Freud, "The Predisposition to Obsessional Neurosis" [1913], *Collected Papers* (New York: Basic Books, 1959), Vol. II, p. 131.

[3] See, for example, Sigmund Freud, "Character and Anal Erotism" [1908], *Collected Papers, op. cit.*, Vol. II, pp. 45–50; Ernest Jones, "Anal-erotic Character Traits" [1918], *Papers on Psychoanalysis* (Baltimore: William Wood, 1938), pp. 531–55; Karl Abraham, "Contributions to the Theory of the Anal Character" [1921], *Selected Papers on Psychoanalysis* (New York: Basic Books, 1957), pp. 370–92.

not describe general ways of functioning that would comprise what we call character.

Such a concept of character appeared later, in the character analysis of Wilhelm Reich.[4] According to Reich, the neurotic solution of the infantile instinctual conflict is accomplished by a generalized alteration in functioning, ultimately crystallizing in a neurotic character, and this—"character as a total formation," not merely specific defense operations or the content of specific traits—becomes the object of study, as it was for Reich the focus of therapeutic attention. "Our problem," he says, "is not the content or the nature of this or that character trait, but the origin and meaningful working of the typical mode of reaction in general."[5]

These modes of reaction—for example, "restraint and evenness in living and thinking" in the obsessive-compulsive—could no longer be described exclusively in terms of the earlier drive content. Character forms "cannot be derived from individual impulses like the contents of the character traits; they give the individual his particular stamp."[6]

These are not only generalized forms of functioning, but also stable, even ossified ones. The ego is "hardened," defenses are consolidated in these forms, and earlier conflict is "transformed into chronic attitudes, into chronic automatic modes of reaction."[7] In this view, therefore, the modes of functioning are detached from the content of the infantile conflict, which is their presumed origin, and achieve, in this respect at least, an autonomy or independence from that original conflict, a feature that is critical to the concept of generalized forms of functioning.[8]

---

[4] Wilhelm Reich, *Character Analysis* [1933] (New York: Orgone Institute Press, 1949).

[5] *Ibid.*, p. 144.

[6] *Ibid.*, p. 196.

[7] *Ibid.*, p. 156.

[8] That this concept is *not* equivalent to Heinz Hartmann's concept of

There are two points, however, at which Reich's picture of character is not adequate, and these two points are closely related. The first concerns the origin of the general mode of reaction or character form, and the second concerns its function. Character, in his view, arises wholly out of the infantile instinctual conflict, originally as a way of mastering that conflict. The factors that determine the particular nature of the character form are the nature of the impulse frustrated, on the one hand, and the nature (extent, time, intensity, and the like) of the frustration, on the other.[9] Once hardened, character continues to have an exclusively defensive (and protective) function. It "binds" impulses in stable ways, limits flexibility, and constitutes an armor against the external world as well as the inner one; in other words, it performs defensive functions in a more economical way than specific defense reactions. While it no longer merely performs the function of mastery over the original conflict, it continues to perform the most essential defensive and protective functions required by the "continuing actual conflict" between instinctual demands and external frustration. Reich said that "the continuing actual conflicts between instinct and outer world give it [the character armor] its strength and continued reason for existence." [10]

Thus, Reich does not take the step of conceiving of general forms with a stable existence independent of defensive requirements or instinctual conflict. Such a picture does not take cogni-

---

"secondary autonomy" (Heinz Hartmann, "Comments on the Psychoanalytic Theory of the Ego," in Ruth S. Eissler et al., eds., The Psychoanalytic Study of the Child, Vol. 5 [New York: International Universities Press, 1950], pp. 74–96) will become clear in the following paragraph.

[9] Reich does admit of constitutional factors other than instinctual ones playing some part in the development of character forms—"even the newborn infant has its 'character' " (ibid., p. 156)—but this suggestion is clearly a concession to an antagonistic viewpoint. He was arguing at that time for an environmental determination of character pathology and against a hereditary concept.

[10] Ibid., p. 146.

zance of characteristic modes of functioning in the adaptive relationship with the external world or in expressiveness. It excludes, among the possible determinants of the shape of character or character forms, the psychological equipment, capacities, or tendencies (such as various cognitive apparatuses and tendencies) that may have been present from the beginning and independent of instinctual conflict. Nor is there any indication, in this view, that external reality—particularly, early social reality—contributes in an essential way to the adaptive development of characteristic modes by way of its own opportunities, demands, and forms. These possibilities were introduced into psychoanalytic theory later, most notably by Heinz Hartmann and Erik H. Erikson.

After Reich, however, direct psychoanalytic interest in the problem of character seems to have diminished. Perhaps, further interest required additional theoretical equipment and new concepts. In any case, the study of the ego, which Reich's work already reflected and undoubtedly advanced, has since moved into the center of general psychoanalytic interest. Along with this, there have been certain developments that bear significantly on our subject. I have three developments in mind: (1) Hartmann's[11] concepts, enlarging on a suggestion in Freud's later writing, of sources of psychological structures independent of instinctual drives and drive conflicts; (2) Erikson's[12] work, which implements such concepts of sources of psychological structures independent of (but still closely coordinated with) instinctual drives and additionally proposes a new concept of generalized modes of functioning; (3) the experimental and theoretical work of George S. Klein,[13] Riley Gardner,[14] and their

---

[11] Heinz Hartmann, *Ego Psychology and the Problem of Adaptation* (New York: International Universities Press, 1958).

[12] Erik H. Erikson, *Childhood and Society* (New York: Norton, 1950).

[13] George S. Klein, "Cognitive Control and Motivation," *Assessment of Motives*, ed. Gardner Lindzey (New York: Rinehart, 1959), pp. 87–118.

[14] Riley Gardner, Philip S. Holzman, George S. Klein, Harriet Linton,

associates, which examines modes and styles of cognition as rep
resentations of general control principles. These three sources,
none of them principally concerned with the subject of character, contribute to a conception of general, stable modes of functioning that is essential for a re-examination of pathological
character.

Hartmann has explored and brought to our attention the significance for psychological development of constitutionally
given mental endowments and apparatuses (for example, memory and perceptual apparatuses). These apparatuses comprise,
Hartmann points out, basic human adaptive equipment and
form the nucleus of a sphere of adaptive psychological functioning that is relatively independent of instinctual conflict. But
these innate endowments and their maturational products (for
example, thinking and language) are not only of significance for
adaptive functioning. According to their individual distribution
and special characteristics, they influence not only the form or
special tendency of later adaptive functioning, but also the form
of or "preference" for ways of handling conflict, ways of defense. For example, Hartmann cites the autonomous factor of
intelligence as an independent codeterminer of the individual
choice and success of the defensive process of intellectualiza-
tion.[15]

It hardly needs to be said that this conception in no way min-
imizes the influence on the forms of defensive or adaptive processes of external, particularly social factors or of instinctual
drives and drive conflicts. But we have in this conception—and
psychoanalysis did not have it before—a biologically rooted nucleus of psychological structure that influences characteristic
form tendencies of both adaptive and defensive functioning

---

and Donald P. Spence, "Cognitive Control: A Study of Individual Consistencies in Cognitive Behavior," *Psychological Issues*, I, Whole No. 4
(1959).

[15] Hartmann, *op. cit.*, p. 14.

from the beginning, a nucleus around which other forces and influences assert themselves and accumulate.

The concept of independent sources of the ego and of ego development that is described by Hartmann in a theoretical and general way is given specific content by Erikson.[16] If Hartmann's work suggests a broader base than was available before for a picture of character development and the development of general forms of functioning, Erikson offers an explicit picture of how such development proceeds, in certain areas at least. Erikson describes the progressive unfolding of general modes of functioning—"patterns of going at things, modes of approach, modes of seeking relationships" [17]—along with psychosexual development, in each phase modeled after the dominant instinctual mode but determined also by concurrently emerging maturational capacities and tendencies. The result of a developmental phase is not merely a matter of the fate of the instinct, but—as the mode is crystallized into socially provided forms (modalities)—it is a way of functioning, an attitude, and a frame of mind. Thus, the phase that can be described psychosexually as "phallic" corresponds to a general expansion of locomotor capacities and "ambulatory and intrusive patterns" [18] and may be more generally described as characterized by the dominance of the intrusive mode, resulting in the establishment of an attitude of initiative (or the impairment of that attitude by guilt).

Thus, in contrast to Reich's "modes of reaction," the general forms of functioning in Erikson's scheme have three roots: instinctual development, the unfolding of maturational capacities and tendencies, and the external social forms that society provides at each developmental phase.

Erikson's modes and modalities, encompassing as much as

---

[16] See David Rapaport, "Present-Day Ego Psychology," lecture given at San Francisco, 1956.

[17] Erikson, *op. cit.*, p. 65.

[18] *Ibid.*, p. 85.

they do, are capable of describing molar aspects of individual functioning in a unique way. They can describe what people do and how people feel, in distinction to what forces drive them or what internal institutions inhibit them. I will return later to this feature of such general modes. Erikson has not attempted a systematic characterology[19] based on the development of these modes, nor has he systematically and in detail related them to existing psychiatric conditions. Although there is little doubt that such a systematic study would be extremely valuable, it is likely that many areas of psychological functioning that are significant for a study of psychopathology—such as cognitive processes—cannot adequately be described by the modes and modalities of Erikson's scheme.

White[20] has argued that, to do justice to a great many types and areas of psychological functioning, Erikson's general modes of functioning are too closely linked to or modeled after libidinal development. It is true that speaking of cognition as intrusive or receptive would not do justice to the processes that are involved, processes of perception, thought, and so on; these terms can describe such processes only in their most behavioral and general aspect. But there is no reason to assume that a single mode must be reproduced in all areas and on all levels of functioning. If, for example, behavior may be described in its psychosexual or social aspects as intrusive, it does not necessarily follow that a mode of cognition that may be completely consistent with intrusive behavior, that may facilitate it and be coordinated with it, is best describable as intrusive. On the contrary, it

---

[19] Such a characterology could not, in any case, be of the sort that was previously envisaged, namely, a reduction of the adult character to its presumed infantile prototype, since ego development continues, in Erikson's view, when psychosexual development is complete. Nevertheless, one or another phase of development may still have been of decisive importance in the determination of adult character.

[20] Robert W. White, "Competence and the Psychosexual Stages of Development," *Nebraska Symposium on Motivation*, ed. Marshall R. Jones (Lincoln: University of Nebraska Press, 1960), pp. 97–141.

is reasonable to assume that we will need to study a number of forms or modes of functioning, describing each in terms appropriate to its own content, these modes themselves interrelated and mutually facilitative.

The work of Klein, Gardner, and their associates is primarily concerned with cognitive functioning, and it is in this work, sharing the general theoretical orientation of Hartmann and Erikson, that a psychological and psychoanalytic concept of style or form of functioning is most clearly developed and applied. Shortly after World War II, there appeared a body of experimental work in the field of perception usually identified by the term "new look." These experiments demonstrated the influence of motive or need on perception. Coming somewhat later and partly in response to the "new look" results, Klein's work showed that the effects of need or motive on perception are not simple and direct ones. Such influences are different in different people, he demonstrated, and, furthermore, the nature of such influences or the particular directions they take are consistent for individuals through a variety of cognitive tasks and in various motivational states. Thus, in an experiment in which thirsty subjects were shown stimuli containing thirst-related themes, cognitive deviations, as compared with nonthirsty subjects, were generally produced; but the deviations were of different sorts among the subjects and were consistent in their direction with cognitive tendencies previously observed when the subjects were not thirsty.[21] It is possible, in other words, to demonstrate that individuals possess relatively stable cognitive tendencies that determine the form of the influence that a motive or need exerts on their cognition.

Klein and his collaborators have investigated a number of these cognitive attitudes. They have conceived of them as regulatory or control structures of considerable generality. The cog-

---

[21] Klein, "Need and Regulation," *Nebraska Symposium on Motivation*, ed. Marshall R. Jones (Lincoln: University of Nebraska Press, 1954), pp. 224–74.

nitive attitudes, Klein writes, "seem to reflect highly generalized forms of control, as likely to appear in a person's perceptual behavior as in his manner of recall and recollection." [22]

Klein considers that a variety of such attitudes are available to an individual and has used the expression "cognitive style" to refer to the total arrangement of them in a given person. These cognitive controls, Klein has suggested,[23] may have a basis in constitutional givens of the sort to which Hartmann referred. The question of the relationship of such controls or styles to defenses, which are the regulatory structures best known to psychoanalysis thus far, has been discussed by Klein to some extent, but it remains to be fully considered. I shall return to this question in the last chapter, but it may be said at this point that individual cognitive styles must certainly be one aspect of the matrix that determines the nature of the specific defense and the shape of the pathological symptom.

Philip Rieff, in Freud: The Mind of the Moralist,[24] has criticized Freud's psychological system for its lack of recognition of contemporary attitudes, tendencies, or "forms of the mind" in their own right. Rieff has in mind, as an example of such contemporary tendencies, the general perceptual tendencies investigated by the Gestalt psychologists. Freud commits the error, Rieff maintains, of identifying contemporary attitudes or character traits with their presumed origin. He argues that "while an oak does originate in an acorn, the mature tree cannot be held to be still 'essentially' acornish." [25] This criticism is justifiable to a significant extent in my opinion, and it may be that the lack that Rieff points to, of "forms of the mind," or, as I would say,

---

[22] George S. Klein, op. cit., p. 89.

[23] As quoted by David Rapaport, "Psychoanalytic Theory of Motivation," Nebraska Symposium on Motivation, ed. Marshall R. Jones (Lincoln: University of Nebraska Press, 1960), p. 219.

[24] Philip Rieff, Freud: The Mind of the Moralist (New York: Viking, 1959).

[25] Rieff, op. cit., p. 49. Rieff's is not a criticism of a historical or genetic point of view as such.

contemporary modes and styles of functioning, is largely responsible for the present-day lack of a psychoanalytic psychology of character. At the same time, it must be added that the deficiency was never as complete as Rieff implies and that the development by Freud of a theory of the ego and of a structural point of view, which led directly to the later developments I have indicated, were steps toward correcting this deficiency.

In any case, I have attempted to show that some general picture of what such "forms of the mind" may consist of, and a groundwork, however fragmentary it may yet be, for an understanding of character is now available. It is clear that the problem of the origins and sources of forms or styles of functioning is not a simple one; much already suggests that they must be products of multiple and interacting sources. I will have little to say about the possible origins of the neurotic styles to be discussed here, except for certain general points in the last chapter. Careful study of the styles themselves and a clearer, more detailed picture of the forms of cognition, activity, emotional experience, and so on, that characterize various pathological conditions is, I am convinced, an indispensable prerequisite to an understanding of origins. Such a study must include careful observation and analysis of the tendencies present in the more or less continuously manifest, perhaps mundane, and ordinarily unremarkable dimensions of experience and activity—the continuous ways of living, conscious attitudes, and overt behavior—and this is essentially what I shall attempt here.[26]

I would like to turn now to the clinical significance of neurotic styles and to certain additional features of what may be called a "formal" view of neurosis.

Freud taught us that even the strangest symptoms and most

---

[26] Cf. Hartmann: "It is . . . natural that pure phenomenological description of the details of the mental superficies, which we could disregard previously, is essential for and attains a special importance in ego psychology" (op. cit., pp. 6–7).

bizarre behavior "make sense." We feel secure now in assuming
that such strangeness is only apparent, and, when the story is
known, what seemed strange will become plausible and even appear inevitable. Perhaps the foremost among the discoveries that
gave this assumption credibility was the discovery of the significance of early instinctual drives. These were the forces that
could be discovered—distorted or redirected but nevertheless
present—behind what seemed bizarre, and the detection of
these forces reduced the bizarre to the simply human. Agencies
responsible for the distortions have always been recognized,
Rieff to the contrary notwithstanding, but they have been recognized in order to discover the universal human forces hidden
by them. However, in recent years, in the study of what has
been called "ego psychology," interest has turned to these agencies themselves, and we ask, How does the individual operate?
as well as, What motivates him? This is not only a theoretical
question, but also an important clinical one. Its answer can
make sense of an additional dimension of neurosis.

Consider an analogy. Suppose we observe an Indian, whose
culture is unfamiliar, performing a strange dance with great intensity. As we watch, puzzled, we may notice that there is a
drought and that this is an agricultural community; we consider
the possibility that this is a prayerful dance designed to bring
rain and that possibly it is an expression of apprehension as well.
By careful observation, we may be able to decipher certain regular gestures that confirm our guess. There is no doubt that, at
this point, we have achieved a significant measure of understanding. But the limitations of that understanding become apparent if we only consider that nearby, watching, is a non-Indian
farmer who also suffers from the drought but does not join in
the dancing. It does not occur to him to perform these gestures;
instead, he goes home and worries. *The Indian dances not only
because there is a drought, but also because he is an Indian.* His
dancing follows from certain attitudes and ways of thinking, a
frame of mind that is likely to be long standing and relatively

stable. Knowledge of these stable forms adds another dimension of plausibility, of sense, to his behavior.

Much the same sort of thing can be said of the neurotic's symptoms or pathological traits. The compulsive person, for instance, is interested in doubts, worries, and rituals. Dynamic understanding, no matter how correct in itself, cannot explain this particular form of his interest. He performs his rituals not only because of the balance of instinctual and counterinstinctual forces, but also because he is a compulsive person, that is, because he is a person with certain relatively stable ways of thinking and cognition, certain attitudes, and so on. And it is not only those ways of functioning that directly have to do with action, plan, or discharge of impulse that are pertinent here, but also ways of experiencing impulse, need or affect. We may assume, in other words, that the compulsive person behaves in the manner that he does, under the impact of a given impulse or external provocation, not only because of certain modes of response or activity, but also because of certain modes of experiencing or perceiving that impulse or stimulus. These are the matters to which a clinical study of neurotic styles must address itself. Such stable and general forms of functioning are responsible for the individual's personal transformation of instinctual impulse or external stimulus into conscious subjective experience, manifest behavior, or overt symptom.[27]

The question of the choice of neurosis, therefore, is of more than theoretical interest. If we are in the dark about the ways of functioning from which that choice follows, we are in the dark about a good deal of the individual's subjective world. It is only in the context of this subjective world or of these ways of functioning that the individual significance of any given mental con-

---

[27] This point is emphasized in Alfred Adler's psychology also, according to which the subjective significance of events will depend on the individual "style of life." But in this conception, as I understand it, "style" is purposive and means the way of living the individual adopts to achieve his life goals.

tent can be clearly understood. A mental content or an item of manifest behavior—a fantasy or a symptom, for instance—not only reflects the content of an instinctual impulse or counterimpulse, but also it is a product of a style of functioning. It is only when we understand the style and the general tendency of the individual's mind and interest that we can reconstruct the subjective meaning of the content of an item of behavior or thought. The same mental content or behavior will have different significance to different individuals, and different contents will have closely similar significance. Without this understanding, we run the risk—and it holds for therapists and testers alike —of seeing only textbook meanings, possibly correct but far removed from the sense and tone of an individual's experience. I do not mean to suggest that we have been completely without such understanding, but only that a formal point of view can be applied to it explicitly and consistently.

There is one other feature of this view of neurosis that I would like to indicate. This feature is a conception of "activeness" in neurotic functioning, a conception that is at variance with some psychiatric understanding. Let me explain what I mean.

One cannot study neurotic styles of functioning without being impressed by the fact that what the neurotic person does and the special way in which he does it, his conscious attitudes and the way he sees things, are essential functional parts of the neurosis. He seems to think in such a way and his attitudes and interests are such as to continue and sustain the neurotic process and to make the characteristic neurotic experiences inevitable, however discomforting they may be. This is not to say, certainly, that he does this by choice or that he can be talked out of it. It simply says that his makeup and the way he sees things—about which he has no choice—move him to feel, think, and do things that continue the neurotic experience and are indispensable to it.

Certain examples of this are generally familiar. We know, for instance, that there are certain angry, guarded, masochistic individuals who seem not only to feel humiliated and victimized easily, but also to be alert for opportunities to be so. They sometimes seem to go far out of their way to seize a chance to feel victimized. It is sometimes possible to understand their interest and their satisfaction in this: each new injustice scores a moral point against the enemy. Most people can understand such an interest, but most people do not find it so compelling. Why, then, do some? Often these people feel embattled more or less continuously, and with a superior foe. Against that enemy, the only weapon is moral protest. They feel extremely aware, from a position of weakness, of relative power and position, of who treats whom with how much respect. They become militantly principled about personal justice and keenly interested in it. According to the personal world constructed by these attitudes and concerns, an objectively remote possibility of affront stares *them* in the face, and only a fool would *not* recognize it. In other words, according to the attitudes and frame of mind of these people, alertness to the possibility of humiliation or mistreatment and "recognition" of instances of it is the only plausible thing to do.

In general, the neurotic's attitudes and interests will be of a sort that guarantees that the next neurotic act—which from an objective standpoint may sustain and continue the neurotic process—will appear as the only plausible next thing to do.[28]

Thus, to mention other examples, the obsessional person, on close examination, is not simply assailed by doubts and worries; he goes out of his way to find a basis for uncertainty, being sure, whenever a decision seems imminent, to find something that will again balance the scales. His attitudes and ways of thinking guarantee that just such a procedure will seem the only prudent

---

[28] This view of the "activeness" of neurotic functioning is very clearly recognized in Hellmuth Kaiser's therapeutic ideas. See Hellmuth Kaiser, "The Problem of Responsibility in Psychotherapy," *Psychiatry*, 18, No. 3 (1955), 205–211.

and proper one and that the next element of doubt will appear as the obvious next thing to be interested in. Similarly, the paranoid person is not simply visited by apprehensions and defensive suspicions; he searches actively and does not rest until he has located clues to new dangers. The repressive person, not only is subject to forces that oppose clear recollection, but also mistakably shrinks from facts when they are offered, prefers to move on to the next subject, or sees no reason for being "so serious." And so on. From this viewpoint, therefore, the neurotic person does not simply suffer neurosis, as, essentially, one suffers tuberculosis or a cold, but actively participates in it, functions, so to speak, according to it, and, in ways that sustain it's characteristic experiences; he sees, at any point, no serious alternative to whatever particular act or interest has just this effect.

Psychoanalysis, in its early phase, did not regard individual functioning in this way, but was inclined to see the conscious individual as either passively moved by libidinal forces[29] or protected, but still passively, from the demands of these forces by the defense mechanisms. Erikson says:

Early psychoanalysis . . . describes human motivation as if libido were the prime substance, individual egos being merely defensive buffers and vulnerable layers between this substance and a vague surrounding "outer world." . . . While we must continue to study the life cycles of individuals by delineating the possible vicissitudes of their libido, we must become sensitive to the danger of forcing living persons into the role of marionettes of a mythical Eros—to the gain of neither therapy nor theory.[30]

This marionette concept does not follow inevitably from the assumption or the study of instinctual drives or unconscious

---

[29] This view is epitomized in Georg Groddeck's famous dictum that we are "lived" by unknown and uncontrollable forces. See reference in Sigmund Freud, *The Ego and the Id* (London: The Hogarth Press, 1950), p. 27.

[30] Erikson, *op. cit.*, p. 60.

forces; it reflects, rather, an insufficient appreciation of the operation of the ego and, perhaps, particularly of consciousness. Possibly, too, it reflects too exclusive a concern with intrapsychic departments, institutions, and forces. This view has been significantly modified by present concepts of ego functioning and, no doubt, will be further modified by further study of consciousness; of attention, thinking, and perception; of intentionality, volitional action, and the like. Nevertheless, the marionette concept is very much present in psychiatric and psychoanalytic thought today, and the basic question of the passiveness or activeness of the neurotic person in relation to his neurosis is still with us.

The issue seems to appear, for instance, in a certain misconception of the meaning of determinism in psychology, as when psychological determinism is taken to imply that the neurotic person is moved by or in the grip of forces that result in manifest behavior of which he is merely a passive witness. The same issue comes up in connection with the understanding of historical (childhood) causes of behavior, where the marionette view suggests that pieces of history intrude themselves into the contemporary behavior of the individual, bypassing his contemporary modes of functioning and leaving him, again, as a passive witness of his own manifest behavior and the victim of his history. Let me emphasize that the question here is not about psychological determinism, historical causation, or unconscious motives; the question concerns the bypassing of consciousness and contemporary modes of functioning, which these views imply. From our point of view, the neurotic person is no longer merely a victim of historical events in the sense described; his way of thinking and his attitudes—his style, in other words—having also been formed by that history, are now integral parts of that neurotic functioning and move him to think, feel, and act in ways that are indispensable to it.

It is worth noting that the marionette viewpoint runs into a particular kind of clinical difficulty with certain sorts of patients, usually impulsive characters or alcoholics who tell us about themselves just what this viewpoint tells us, namely, that they are victims of their impulses or that they "can't help it." We may feel a certain confusion on hearing this. In some sense, these patients must be right; our understanding of determinism tells us so, and we wish to avoid the apparent alternative of placing a moral onus on neurosis. On the other hand, we cannot quite swallow the idea of their innocence and cannot help noticing that they do not altogether regret what their impulses choose to do with them. The marionette concept causes some therapists to feel they are under a scientific obligation to accept such disclaimers of responsibility at face value, while others may be moved to moralistic attitudes in spite of themselves. Examination of this style will show that what these people really cannot help is their inclination, under certain circumstances of motivation, to feel, "I can't help it," an attenuation of normal experience of volition that is an aspect of the general impulsive style.

I believe that this general view of neurosis emerges consistently from the examination of neurotic styles and, in a consistent way, only from such an examination. But I would like to stress again that the study of the styles themselves is my principal aim. The reader will decide for himself whether the facts of the study bring him to the same conclusions.

Obsessive-Compulsive Style

Wilhelm Reich described compulsive characters as "living machines." [1] It is an apt description and one that is, in fact, confirmed in the subjective experience of some of these people (see p. 40). It is, also, a good example of a general formal description. This machinelike quality is not to be derived from the content of any instinctual impulse nor from any mental content.

Many formal characteristics of obsessive-compulsive functioning are, in fact, quite familiar, probably more than for any of the other neurotic conditions. For example, we are familiar with a distinctive way of thinking marked by "rigidity," a certain mode of tense activity, and the like. Obsessive-compulsive people also show, in their intellectuality, what is probably the most familiar example of a formal characteristic with both conspicuous defensive and adaptive aspects. However, the fact that such traits are well known by no means necessarily indicates that their formal characteristics are well understood or have been seriously studied. For example, I know of no study of obsessive-compulsive intellectual rigidity, although it is certainly one of the most easily observed psychiatric phenomena. And this is true despite the

---

[1] Wilhelm Reich, *Character Analysis* [1933] (New York: Orgone Institute Press, 1949), p. 199.

fact that the obsessive-compulsive neurosis has been the subject of the most intensive study from a dynamic standpoint, that is, from the standpoint of the instinctual and counterinstinctual forces involved in it.

I have selected three aspects of the obsessive-compulsive style of functioning for examination: (1) rigidity, (2) the mode of activity and the distortion of experience of autonomy, and (3) the loss of reality. The first and third aspects are primarily those of cognition and thinking. The second refers to the sort of activity we often describe as "driven" and to aspects of the obsessive-compulsive's most characteristic form of subjective experience; this section comes closest, perhaps, to describing the obsessive-compulsive's way of living in general.

Rigidity

The term "rigidity" is frequently used to describe various characteristics of obsessive-compulsive people. It may refer, for example, to a stiff body posture, a stilted social manner, or a general tendency to persist in a course of action that has become irrelevant or even absurd. But, above all, "rigidity" describes a style of thinking.

What exactly is meant by rigidity of thinking? Consider as a commonplace example the sort of thinking one encounters in a discussion with a compulsive, rigid person, the kind of person we also call "dogmatic" or "opinionated." Even casual conversation with such a person is often very frustrating, and it is so for a particular reason. It is not simply that one meets with unexpected opposition. On the contrary, such discussion is typically frustrating just because one experiences neither real disagreement nor agreement. Instead, there is no meeting of minds at all, and the impression is simply of not being heard, of not receiving any but perfunctory attention. The following excerpt from a conversation will illustrate the point. Two friends, K and L, are discussing the buying of a house in which K is interested.

K: So you think I shouldn't buy it?
L: Never buy a house with a bad roof. It will cost you its price
    again in repairs before you're finished.
K: But the builder I hired to look it over did say it was in good
    condition otherwise.
L: The roof is only the beginning. First it's the roof and then
    comes the plumbing and then the heating and then the plaster.
K: Still, those things seem to be all right.
L: And, after the plaster, it will be the wiring.
K: But the wiring is. . . .
L: [interrupts with calm assurance] It will cost double the price
    before you're finished.

In this illustration, L does not exactly disagree with K. He
does not actually object to or oppose K's arguments, and he cannot be called "negativistic." He simply does not pay attention.
This is an inattention, furthermore, that has a special quality; it
is quite different, for instance, from the wandering attention of
a tired person. This inattention seems somehow to have an active and, as it were, a principled quality. It is in just such inattention to new facts or a different point of view that rigidity (or
its more specific form, dogmatism) in the obsessive-compulsive
person seems to manifest itself. It is this inattention that makes
us experience these people as being so utterly uninfluencible.
Without defining it further for the time being, let me say,
therefore, that some kind of special restriction of attention
seems to be one crucial feature of obsessive-compulsive intellectual rigidity, although not necessarily the only one.

It may clarify this feature, as well as others, of the compulsive's rigidity to consider the fact that intellectual rigidity is not
peculiar to obsessive-compulsive people. Specifically, quite dramatic forms of such rigidity are often observed in cases of organic brain damage. This comparison may seem a strange one,
but it is valid enough. The phenomena described by the term
"rigidity" in these two types of pathology do in fact have essential features in common. I would like to digress briefly to examine certain features of thought rigidity in organic cases, where

it is certainly more vivid and, on the whole, better understood than in obsessive-compulsives.

Goldstein[2] and others have shown that the rigidity of the organically brain-damaged person is an aspect of the concrete, "stimulus-bound" quality of their cognition and general mode of approach. The organically brain-damaged person's attention appears to be gripped or passively held by a more or less immediately manifest or concrete aspect of a situation or task (or by an aspect that has been otherwise imposed on his attention), and he cannot detach himself from it. His attention, held by one aspect of a situation or task, can be distracted, that is, it can be pulled away, but he is not able to shift it himself. He has, in other words, lost the capacity for volitional direction of attention.

For example, "A patient who has just succeeded in reciting the days of the week is now asked to recite the alphabet. He cannot shift to this task, and only after repeated promptings, or better stated, after the examiner has commenced to call out the alphabet, can the patient follow in his recitation. . . . Another patient can call out the number series from one on, but if the examiner asks him to begin with a number other than one, the patient is at a loss, he must start with one." [3]

The normal person, in contrast, has the capacity *not* to be gripped, the capacity to detach himself from the concrete or immediately manifest features of a situation or task and to shift his attention smoothly and rapidly, now to this aspect, now to that aspect. He has the capacity for volitional direction of attention.

What I am describing here is, of course, what we call "flexibility." I am suggesting that cognitive flexibility may be described

---

[2] Kurt Goldstein and Martin Scheerer, "Abstract and Concrete Behavior: An Experimental Study with Special Tests," *Psychological Monographs*, LIII (1941), Whole No. 2.

[3] Goldstein and Scheerer, *ibid.*, p. 5.

as a mobility of attention of this sort, a volitional mobility of attention. Now, we concluded before that obsessive-compulsive intellectual rigidity, also, was characterized by some special limitation of attention. Can we say that, notwithstanding the obvious disparity between the obsessive-compulsive's and the brain-damaged person's rigidity, they have this feature in common: that both are characterized by some general loss or impairment of volitional mobility of attention?

Although the obsessive-compulsive's attention certainly cannot be described as stimulus-bound or flagrantly unable to shift volitionally, as in the brain-damaged person, it is in fact, far from being free and mobile. Let me describe this mode of attention and its limitations more closely.

The most conspicuous characteristic of the obsessive-compulsive's attention is its intense, sharp focus. These people are not vague in their attention. They concentrate, and particularly do they concentrate on detail. This is evident, for example, in the Rorschach test in their accumulation, frequently, of large numbers of small "detail-responses" and their precise delineation of them (small profiles of faces all along the edges of the inkblots, and the like), and the same affinity is easily observed in everyday life. Thus, these people are very often to be found among technicians; they are interested in, and at home with, technical details. The same sharpness of attention is, of course, also an aspect of many obsessive-compulsive symptoms. They will notice a bit of dust or worry over some insignificant inaccuracy that, everything else aside, simply would not gain the attention of another person. But the obsessive-compulsive's attention, although sharp, is in certain respects markedly limited in both mobility and range. These people not only concentrate; they seem always to be concentrating. And some aspects of the world are simply not to be apprehended by a sharply focused and concentrated attention. Specifically, this is a mode of attention that seems unequipped for the casual or immediate impression, that more passive and impressionistic sort of cognitive experience that can include in its notice or allow one to be "struck" by even that which is peripheral or incidental to its original, intended focus of attention or that may not even possess a clear intention or sharp focus in the first place. These people seem unable to allow their attention simply to wander or passively permit it to be captured. Thus, they rarely seem to get hunches, and they are rarely struck or surprised by anything. It is not that they do not look or listen, but they are looking or listening too hard for something else.

For example, these people may listen to a recording with the keenest interest in, and attention to, the quality of the equipment, the technical features of the record, and the like, but meanwhile hardly hear, let alone are captured by, the music.

In general, the obsessive-compulsive person will have some sharply defined interest and will stick to it; he will go after and get the facts—and will get them straight—but he will often miss those aspects of a situation that give it its flavor or its impact. Thus, these people often seem quite insensitive to the "tone" of social situations. In fact—such is the human capacity to make a virtue of a necessity—they often refer with pride to their singlemindedness or imperturbability.

The sharp but narrowed focus of the obsessive-compulsive's mode of attention, then, misses certain aspects of the world even while it engages others quite successfully. Not every mode of cognition that is capable of intense concentration and sharply focused attention suffers these limitations. Some people are able to regard the casual impression with a casual attention, to entertain the hunch, to notice the element on the periphery of attention briefly, in other words, and then pass on (or not) with greater or lesser gain. This is a free mobility of attention, a flexible cognitive mode. But the obsessive-compulsive person is not so equipped. For him the hunch or the passing impression is only a potential distraction, and a discomforting one at that, from his single-minded concentration. And he seems to avoid that distraction exactly by the intensity of his sharp, narrow focus of attention. Let me explain this further.

We are not born with the ability to concentrate intensely, to look or listen technically, sharply, and intently for something, or to keep our mind's eye focused keenly on a single point for a long period of time and, as we say, follow a train of thought. The cognition of childhood is highly impressionistic and distractible; the child's attention is, at it were, open and ready to be captured. Those active and normally volitional cognitive capacities, such as the capacity for intense and sustained concentration, in which the obsessive-compulsive excels are capacities that mature slowly in childhood [4] and quite possibly continue developing even into adolescence. Probably these capacities for volitional direction of attention develop, at least in their initial phases, along with the development of other capacities for volitional direction, including muscular direction, and of intentionality in general. At any rate, in the normal case these cognitive capacities *are* achieved; direction and maintenance of attention *at will* in such forms as sustained concentration becomes possible. Normally, in fact, these capacities for intense and sharply focused attention become sufficiently well established to permit them to be activated and relaxed at will and so smoothly as to be hardly noticeable. The normal person, in other words, can concentrate *and* entertain a hunch, and he can allow his attention to shift not only in direction, but also in intensity and can do all this smoothly. In some cases, however—and the obsessive-compulsive is one, although not the only one—this directedness of attention seems to be maintained, and is apparently maintainable, only under continuous tension, with great intensity and extreme narrowness of focus—in other words, in a continuous, rigid, and in some respects hypertrophied form.

We are, then, entitled to say that this cognitive mode does

---

[4] Ernest G. Schachtel, *Metamorphosis* (New York: Basic Books, 1959). See particularly Chapter 11, "The Development of Focal Attention and the Emergence of Reality," pp. 251–78.

involve an impairment of the normal volitional mobility of attention. The normal capacity for smooth and volitional shifts between a sharply directed and a more relaxed, impressionistic cognition is absent here. Elements on the periphery of attention, the new or the surprising, that which can only be apprehended impressionistically—all these are only potentially distracting and disruptive to the obsessive-compulsive, and they are avoided exactly by the intensity and the fixed narrowness of his preoccupation with his own idea or aim. It is like shooting an arrow on a windy day; the greater the tension of the bow and force of the arrow, the less susceptible the arrow will be to incidental winds. This is what we mean by the obsessive-compulsive's intellectual rigidity and what we experience as a quality of "active inattention" to any external influence or any new idea on the part of the compulsive dogmatic person. It will, also, be understandable from this view of obsessive-compulsive cognition that the same qualities that make these people seem so rigid in one context endow them, in another, with excellent technical facility and an impressive capacity for concentration on a technical problem.

The Mode of Activity and the General Distortion of the Experience of Autonomy

In each neurotic style, one can describe, in addition to a characteristic cognitive mode, interrelated modes of activity, of affect experience, and the like. But there is no doubt that, among the neurotic styles, there are not only differences in form of functioning within such areas as these, but also differences in the significance the various areas may have in the overall psychological organization. In the hysterical style, for instance, affective experience virtually dominates the individual's existence. In the obsessive-compulsive style, on the other hand, affective experience as a whole shrinks, as will soon become plain; it is in the nature of this style that life pivots around work activity and certain sorts of subjective experience associated with it.

The most conspicuous fact about the activity of the obsessive-compulsive is its sheer quantity and, along with this, its intensity and concentration. These people may be enormously productive in socially recognized ways, or they may not; however that may be, they are, typically, intensely and more or less continuously active at some kind of work. In particular, they are perhaps most typically represented in intensive routine or technical work. In fact, many compulsive symptoms consist of grotesque intensifications of just such activities.

For example, there is the compulsive patient who spends all day intensively cleaning and recleaning the house or the obsessional patient who spends vast amounts of time carefully collecting and transcribing to index cards data on all the schools and colleges he can locate with the dim justification of some day attending "the best."

This basic fact of the more or less continuous absorption of these people in intensive activity of this sort is a significant one, and it is worth noting already that it is a mode of functioning that is well suited to their rigid, technical cognition; but there is another quality about this activity that is equally distinctive. I am speaking now about the special subjective quality of it. The activity—one could just as well say the life—of these people is characterized by a more or less continuous experience of tense deliberateness, a sense of effort, and of trying.

Everything seems deliberate for them. Nothing is effortless. This tense deliberateness or sense of trying cannot be regarded simply as a greater measure of the experience of effort felt by anyone engaged in an activity that in some way taxes his capacities. For the compulsive person, the quality of effort is present in every activity, whether it taxes his capacities or not. Or, to put it more accurately, every activity seems to be carried out in such a way as to tax his capacities. In the area of work, of course, such a quality of effort is generally more expected and, therefore, less noticeable, and there is no doubt that work is the obsessive-compulsive's preferred area of existence. But the effortfulness and tense deliberateness extends also into activities that are, for the normal person, playful or fun. The compulsive person tries just as effortfully to "enjoy" himself at play as he does to accomplish or produce at work.

One such person carefully scheduled his Sundays with certain activities in order to produce "maximum enjoyment" He determinedly set about enjoying himself and became quite upset if anything interfered with his schedule, not merely because he missed the activity, but because his holiday had been spent inefficiently. Another compulsive patient always tried hard, in his social life, to be "spontaneous."

How can we understand the continuous effortfulness, trying, and tense deliberateness of this way of living? How can we distinguish it, aside from its continuousness, from the normal person's effort to do something that taxes him? The normal person's effort, one might say, is hard, whereas the obsessive-compulsive's effort is labored. Let me clarify the distinction further in another way. When the normal person says that he will try to do something, he means that he intends to do his best to do it, but the obsessive-compulsive person does not mean exactly that. When the obsessive-compulsive person says that he will try, he means, not necessarily that he intends to *do* it or do his best to do it, but that he intends to tax himself with the task, admonish himself to do it, and perhaps worry about it. Sometimes, in fact, when he says he will *try*, he has no intention of *doing* it at all.

Thus, a patient announced that she was going to try to stop smoking, and with this announcement she did, indeed, look as if she were making some kind of mental effort. But at the same time she proceeded to take a cigarette out and light it. Clearly her statement did not reflect an intention to stop; it reflected, instead, an intention to achieve a special state of effort or, perhaps, an intention to worry about stopping.

Deliberateness, trying, effort of will are obviously a part of normal psychological life as well as the obsessive-compulsive's. But the object of the normal person's will is, on the whole, something external to himself; he decides to stop smoking. The object of the obsessive-compulsive's will, on the other hand, seems in part at least to be himself; he decides to "try" to stop smoking.

Sometimes the obsessive-compulsive's activity is also described as "driven." No doubt, this description refers partly to the sheer quantity and intensity of his activity, suggesting, I suppose, that no one could possibly work as hard of his own free will. But the term is apt in another sense as well. The compulsive's activity actually has the appearance of being pressed or motivated by something beyond the interest of the acting person. He does not seem that enthusiastic. His genuine interest in the activity, in other words, does not seem to account for the intensity with which he pursues it. Instead he acts, and indeed he feels, as though he were being pressed by some necessity or requirement which he is at pains to satisfy. In actual fact, he *is* pressed by such a necessity or requirement. But it is not an external requirement. It is a requirement and a pressure that he applies to himself.

Thus, these people will frequently give themselves deadlines for various activities, which logically may be quite arbitrary. One patient decided that he must have a better job by his next birthday or else he would have to regard himself as a failure. Of course, he then felt extremely pressed as the day approached, as anyone would given his assumption. With the passing of his birthday, the deadline was shifted to the first of the year, and so on.

If, in other words, we choose to characterize the obsessive-compulsive's activity as driven, then we must also characterize him as the driver. He not only suffers under the pressure of the deadline; he also sets it. And he not only sets it, but also continually reminds himself of its existence and its nearness. He will never complain about this aspect of his behavior, incidentally, nor see it as "neurotic." Although, from an objective standpoint, this attitude is quite critical to the neurotic process, from his standpoint it is only good sense. He will often complain, however, and, in a sense, quite justifiably, about the experience of the pressure itself.

Thus, to speak of the drivenness of obsessive-compulsive activity, on the one hand, or the tense deliberateness and effortfulness of it, on the other, is only to describe variations of the same mode. It is a mode of activity in which the individual exerts a more or less continuous pressure on himself, while at the same time living and working under the strain of that pressure. The obsessive-compulsive person functions like his own overseer issuing commands, directives, reminders, warnings, and admonitions concerning not only what is to be done and what is not to be done, but also what is to be wanted, felt, and even thought. This is the meaning of the single most characteristic thought-content of obsessive-compulsive people: "I should." Depending on its tone, it may be a directive, a reminder, a warning, or an admonition; but in one tone or another, the obsessive-compulsive tells himself, "I should. . . ," almost continuously. I would like to suggest now that this mode of activity and experience reflects a remarkable distortion of the normal function and experience of will or volition, a general distortion comparable to the more specific one that we discussed in connection with the problem of intellectual rigidity.

In the relatively helpless infant, behaving reflexively, pressed from the inside by drives, compelled from the outside by drive objects, one hardly can speak of volition or intentionality, except, possibly, in the most rudimentary sense. In the course of development, however, human beings acquire the capacity for many kinds of volitional activity and function or, in general, the capacity to do things intentionally, deliberately, or at will. This capacity, insofar as it describes an individual's capacity to direct himself, that is, to direct various aspects of his behavior, his actions, his attention to a certain extent, and so on, may also be called a capacity for "autonomous" functioning. I cannot say, and it is not necessary here to attempt it, what kinds of maturational process and equipment are involved in that general development, although we know certain landmarks of it (such as the development of volitional bowel control). Its initial phases must involve not only the development of muscular equipment, but, for example, various cognitive capacities, such as the capacity for anticipation, elementary planning, and so on, which will be essential if the new muscular capacities are to achieve their normal significance and be exercised with their normal competency. In any case, in the course of this development—which probably extends throughout childhood and even adolescence and is not to be wholly identified with any brief developmental phase— much that was originally involuntary becomes supplemented or superseded by volitional behavior. The means of satisfying hunger, eliminative functions, and even ideational and thought processes come to be, at least to some extent, within the domain of intentional direction. This development of the capacity for deliberate and purposeful activity gradually must bring with it many new kinds of psychological experience and new kinds and dimensions of self-awareness. Among these is a new sense of self-direction, autonomy, or choice that we usually describe as the experience of "will," and we are used to seeing in children who are somewhat flush with this new experience that special interest and satisfaction in the exercise of their autonomy that we call "willfulness."

Not every aspect of psychological function and behavior becomes deliberate or comes under willful direction. While the satisfaction of instinctual drives becomes a subject, up to a certain point, of intention and will, the drives themselves never come under the domination of intentionality. It is not in the nature of drives or affects to be called up and banished at will (a fact that compulsive people, when they tell themselves that they "should" feel this way or "should not" feel that way refuse to recognize). In general, while the capacity for willful or volitional choice and action implies an immense enlargement of possibilities of satisfactions and interests, the nature of one's interests, preferences, or feelings is not itself subject to choice or determinable at will. For the normal person, the fact that one sector of life, so to speak, is within the domain of intentionality and volition and another sector is not presents no special problem. If the capacity for volition and the sense of autonomy and will are well established they can also be relaxed to make room for whim, playfulness, spontaneity of affective expression, and the like. A person whose direction of himself is secure can, in other words, afford abandonment of direction of himself in various forms and degrees with neither the expectation nor the fact of disastrous consequences. Altogether, in the normal case, intentionality becomes sufficiently well established to function smoothly, without self-consciousness and, for the most part, without any special tension, and the willfulness of childhood seems to develop into an adult's sense of competency and freedom to do with himself what he chooses.

In certain cases, however, the development of will and volition is achieved only in a markedly distorted and rigid form. The obsessive-compulsive represents one such case, and, as I shall show later, the paranoid represents another. The obsessive-compulsive person lives in a continuous state of volitional tension. We have encountered one aspect of this state in the form of his intellectual rigidity, but it pervades every aspect of his life. In his psychology, self-direction is distorted from its normal meaning of volitional choice and deliberate, purposeful action to a self-conscious directing of his every action, to the exercise, as if by an overseer, of a continuous willful pressure and direction on himself and even, strange as it may appear, an effort to direct his own wants and emotions at will. These people are "willful" with a vengeance. Every action, every direction is weighty, heavy with deliberateness, like an act of state. They not only tolerate no interference with their own willful direction by others, that is, in the sense of being stubborn, but also, embarked on their deliberate course, they tolerate no interference even from themselves. Willful directedness has been distorted from its normal subjective significance as an extension and, so to speak, representative of one's wants to a position of precedence over wants, aimed even at directing them. Impulse, in this order of things, is not the initiator or the first stage of willful directedness and effort, but its enemy. Thus, for these people, impulse or wish is only a temptation which can corrupt their determination, interrupt their work, interfere with what they feel they "should" want to be doing, or otherwise endanger their rigid directedness. They are, therefore, cut off from the sources that normally give willful effort its direction, a fact that has, as will become plain, many consequences.

There are a great many manifestations of this general mode of functioning in the obsessive-compulsive's life, some of them, incidentally, so much a part of our culture, particularly our work culture, that they are taken for granted and hardly excite attention. One important and interesting example of this style of experience and activity is what we call "will power." Will power, so characteristic of the obsessive-compulsive and so adaptable to routine work activity, is comprised exactly of the experience of issuing willful commands and directives to oneself.

This style of activity and experience, it will be clear, also implies a special kind of self-awareness, an awareness of the overseer sitting behind and issuing commands, directives, and reminders, that the obsessive-compulsive person is never without. It is the self-awareness of a person who is working under pressure with a stopwatch in hand. Since, for the obsessive-compulsive, virtually all of life is transformed into such activity, the experience for him is continuous. We see this, for example, in the role-playing that is characteristic of these people. It is important for the obsessive-compulsive person always to be aware that he is a "this" or a "that." This awareness of and interest in establishing his role is an essential step in the transformation of whole areas of living into his characteristic mode. Once his role is established in his mind, it becomes a general directive for behavior, one that is often capable of including even the details of facial expressions, ways of speaking, and the like. Compulsive people are usually especially aware, in this way, of their professional role—the compulsive doctor plays the doctor—or their marital or parental role. They are often aware even of the role of themselves and act it; that is, they have an awareness, in certain respects, of what they are like, and they direct their behavior accordingly. It is this awareness of "role" and acting always under its directive that frequently gives the behavior of these people a stilted quality or a stuffy, pompous one. Fenichel gives a good example of this process, though without indicating its generality.

A patient felt well only as long as he knew what "role" he was supposed to "play." When at work he thought, "I am a worker," and this gave him the necessary security; when at home, "Now I am the husband who comes home from work to his beloved family." [5]

It should be added, however, that in this example it is not simply the *awareness* that is essential to this patient, but rather that the awareness is essential to the *directive* and the whole characteristic mode of activity and experience. Thus, when the patient thinks, "Now I am a worker," he means, also, "Now I should behave according to how workers behave."

Another, modern, example of the same process is the obsessional patient in psychotherapy who is interested in finding out from his

---

[5] Otto Fenichel, *The Psychoanalytic Theory of Neurosis* (New York: Norton, 1945), p. 530.

dreams, fantasies, and so forth, what he "really" thinks, wants, and feels like. Once he finds out, he needs only to direct himself to act that way.

Where, and how, does the obsessive-compulsive person derive these directives, commands, and pressures, the "shoulds" which he issues to himself and under which he then lives? Objectively, there is no doubt that they come from him: *He* reminds himself of his "role," contrives and invokes his deadlines, issues his own commands. But notwithstanding that the authorship and the responsibility for these commands and directives may, objectively, be solely his, he does not feel that they are his. He does not feel that he issues these directives wholly on his own authority and by his own free choice. On the contrary, the obsessive-compulsive always feels that he is reminding himself of some compelling objective necessity, some imperative or higher authority than his personal choice or wish, which he is obliged to serve.

Thus, these people feel that propriety requires them to dress neatly, duty obliges them to visit Aunt Tilly, the boss's expectations make it necessary to finish the job early, health requires a certain amount of calisthenics every day, mental health necessitates a certain number of hobbies and a quantity of "relaxation," culture a certain amount of reading and music, and so on. It does not occur to the compulsive person that to many other people none of these duties and "necessities" carry any weight at all, and if it does occur, no matter—to him they do carry weight.

When the obsessive-compulsive person acts as his own overseer, he also feels that he acts in response to the requirements of some objective necessity, particularly some moral necessity. He feels in the capacity of agent or representative to himself of that objective necessity or imperative. These external pressures or imperatives, which the obsessive-compulsive person endows with such compelling authority, take many forms. These people are keenly aware of various kinds of external expectation, of the threat of possible criticism, of the weight and direction of authoritative opinion, of rules, regulations, and conventions, and, perhaps above all, of a great assemblage of moral or quasi-moral principles. They do not feel literally forced to comply with these, and they do not precisely submit to them. They recognize their authority and press themselves, for example, feel duty-bound, to comply with them.

The necessity to maintain a rigid and continuous state of directed and purposive activity and a continuous pressure on himself requires an experience of this sort, that is, an experience of some compelling necessity or moral imperative superior to his own wishes or choices. This regime of rigid, willful pressure—the regime of effort, in other words—has no intrinsic direction. The obsessive-compulsive stands ready for duty, ready to exercise will power, ready to work or at least to "try," but he must have, in order to function in this way, some authoritative directive to transmit to himself. These people feel and function like driven, hardworking, automatons pressing themselves to fulfill unending duties, "responsibilities," and tasks that are, in their view, not chosen, but simply there.

One compulsive patient likened his whole life to a train that was running efficiently, fast, pulling a substantial load, but on a track laid out for it.

In other words, they do not feel like free men. In fact, they feel exceedingly uncomfortable in circumstances that do offer them a whiff of freedom. This is a common difficulty that obsessive-compulsive people experience on vacations or holidays. On just those occasions when the regular duties, responsibilities, and burdens of work, about which they have complained, are lifted, they show unmistakable signs of discomfort until they have located some new pressure or compelling duty.

One patient frequently expressed the complaint about weekends, "But I don't know what I want to do." He tried to solve the problem by a psychological search of himself, including even his dreams, in order to find out what he "wanted" to do, working on the theory that it was a rule of mental health to do what one wanted to do.

The pressures and directives with which the obsessive-compulsive person lives are beyond doubt extremely burdensome to him, but they are also authoritative guides. They provide a framework within which he can function comparatively comfortably, but outside of which he is extremely discomforted. At work, these people are often most comfortable feeling that they have their own little niche or bailiwick in which they devote themselves to carrying out their established duties ordained by higher authorities. Their choices become narrowed to technical ones—the best way to meet the deadline or satisfy the expectation. Their satisfactions are not the satisfactions of decision and freedom, but the satisfactions of duty for the time being done, authority temporarily pleased, and, frequently, the satisfactions of exercising a highly developed technical virtuosity and ingenuity.

I suggested before that the obsessive-compulsive's experience of imposing on himself and living under a quasi-external pressure and directive is represented by one specific thought-content far more than any other, namely the thought, "I should. . . ." This is the thought with which he drives himself at work, directs himself to behave in certain ways, and even admonishes himself and worries (for example, "I should have . . ." or, "Maybe I should . . ."). Probably this thought or some variation of it (such as "I must," in the same sense) is an explicit part of certain obsessional and compulsive symptoms (for example, "I should wash") and perhaps it is implicit in other symptoms (for example, tics). In one form or another, he is rarely without his "should." In general, the reference of the "should" is to moral principles, and obsessive-compulsive people will find moral considerations in the most remote and unlikely places. But it is important to note that it may also refer to many other kinds of imperative, such as rules of propriety or custom or the bosses expectations. I would like to emphasize this because of the light in which it places the obsessive-compulsive's moral feelings.

The moral aspects of the sense of "should" coincide with what may otherwise be called a superego function. If we consider this superego function in the light of the previous discussion, however, one essential fact emerges. The obsessive-compulsive's moral experience, his moral "should," is only a special content, although an exceedingly important one, of his general and more or less continuous experience of living under and representing to himself a quasi-external pressure. Thus, between such clearcut experience of moral pressure, as in "I should go to church" or "I should be kind to him," and other quite non-moral pressures, such as the pressure of a deadline, "I must get this done before . . ."—there are any number of quasimoral principles, duties, and requirements that, at various times, make up the obsessive-compulsive's experience of pressure and quasi-external directive.

In this general form of subjective experience, therefore, the specifically moral content or superego function appears to lose its distinctness. To be sure, one may easily imagine a specifically moral content as having derived from a more general form of experience, or one may be willing to assign to the superego the general form as a whole, but, in either case, a mental function that one may call "superego" and that is relatively independent of the general mode of existence is difficult to identify. We need not concern ourselves here with this theoretical problem; however, I would like to make one additional point concerning a specific quality that is commonly attributed to the obsessive-compulsive's superego, namely, its "harshness."

The superego of the obsessive-compulsive has often beeen considered to be unusually harsh. It has also, or perhaps alternatively, been described as inadequately integrated. These descriptions, no doubt, are based in part on the evidence of more or less continuous tension or worry, associated with the sense of "should," that appears to plague these people and from which they hardly seem able to escape. Although the phenomena are clear enough, they appear in a somewhat different perspective from the present point of view. If one takes into consideration the nature of the general mode of activity and experience of which the sense of "should" is an aspect, it becomes clear that this quality of "harshness" or "inadequate integration" is absolutely necessary to the whole function of that mode.

When we say that the pressure of the "should" is harsh or poorly integrated, we say essentially that the individual experiences a continuous pressure that seems distinct from and alien to his own wishes. But these are the very conditions that allow him to feel the uncomfortable but ultimately reassuring presence of a command or directive under which he can serve. If the pressure was not "harsh," if it tended, in other words, to merge with what are experienced as free choices or wants, that sense of an external directive would vanish. Thus, it is not surprising that the obsessive-compulsive person ultimately rejects any apparently comforting offer of relief from the "harsh" demands of his conscience, for, from his point of view, such relief promises more loss than gain. On the contrary, when he is temporarily relieved of such demands, for example, on vacations, he immediately looks around for new ones.

Obviously much of life, aside from work, shrinks and is severely restricted in this style of functioning. Certain areas of psychological life simply are not compatible with a continuous, rigid state of deliberate activity or tension. Certain kinds of subjective experience, affect experience particularly, require by their nature an abandonment or at least a relaxation of the attitude of deliberateness, and, where such relaxation is impossible, as in the obsessive-compulsive style, those areas of psychological life tend to shrink. Hence, the dry, mechanical quality or the dull heaviness that frequently characterizes these people. One sometimes witnesses the unhappy spectacle of such a person deliberately attempting to achieve a state of mind or a mood, such as a mood of gaiety, for which a relaxation of such deliberateness is the first prerequisite.

Sometimes this restriction of affect is mistakenly attributed to the obsessive-compulsive's "overcontrol," which suggests that these people can deliberately or by effort of will restrict or otherwise control their own experience of affect or impulse. This, of course, they cannot do, much as they might like to; they can only control to some extent the outward expression of affect. But, although they cannot curb or restrict affect experience *by* deliberate effort, the *existence* of that state of tense deliberateness—and the discomfort, should that deliberateness begin to relax, that moves them to resume it—*automatically* restricts not only affect experience, but also whim, playfulness, and spontaneous action in general.

The discomfort that these people feel in the face of any temptation to relax their attitude of deliberateness, their effortful activity, or their purposefulness takes many specific forms, is expressed in many attitudes, and often involves elaborate rationalizations.

For example, one patient maintained that he must avoid watching any television since he might enjoy it, want to watch more, become addicted to it and want to do nothing else, and then, what would become of the book he was writing?

In general, obsessive-compulsive people feel that any relaxation of deliberateness or purposeful activity is improper, unsafe, or worse. If they are not working, they usually feel that they should at least be thinking (that is, worrying) about some problem, and the prospect of not worrying about a problem that exists, even if it is one that they can do nothing about, seems quite foolhardy to them. They do not feel comfortable with any activity that lacks an aim or a purpose beyond its own pleasure, and usually they do not recognize the possibility of finding life satisfying without a continuous sense of purpose and effort, a continuous sense of advancing the career, making money, writing papers, or the like.

Sometimes obsessive-compulsive people experience an unusual impulse or temptation together with a specific kind of anxiety and discomfort that is worth mentioning here. I am referring to the fear of "going crazy" or, as it is sometimes described, the feeling of "loss of control" that is, at one time or another, quite commonly expressed by these people. It is sometimes assumed that this experience necessarily reflects an actual danger of psychosis, a weakness of defense and an actual pressure of primitive impulse of great intensity. Although sometimes this is no doubt the case, it is by no means invariably so. This fear seems to arise in obsessive-compulsive people when, for whatever reason, their usual rigid deliberateness is significantly interrupted, for example when they are tempted to some unusually abandoned, but by no means necessarily aggressive or primitive, behavior.

Thus, a fear of "losing control" is often experienced, and expressed in therapy hours, by rigid people when they start to laugh very hard or become unusually excited and lose their usual sober composure.

In other words, the experience by these people of an imminent "loss of control" often seems to represent no more than their sensation of a loss or relaxation of volitional tension, a relaxation of "will," and while this is an experience which from their standpoint may seem like "going crazy," it is by no means equivalent to a loss or breakdown of defensive or other such impulse-control structures as would be involved in an actual psychotic episode.

There is another kind of psychological experience that seems to be at least as discomforting to the obsessive-compulsive person as a temporary abandonment to impulse or whim. I am speaking of the process of decision-making. Among the activities of ordinary life, there is probably none for which this style is less suited. No amount of hard work, driven activity, or will power will help in the slightest degree to make a decision. Sometimes the difficulty and discomfort that these people experience when a decision is in prospect is explained as a reflection of their ambivalence. But what distinguishes obsessional people in the face of a decision is not their mixed feelings, but rather the fact that those feelings are always so marvelously and perfectly balanced. In fact, it is easy to observe that just at the moment when an obsessional person seems to be approaching a decision, just when the balance is at last tipping decisively in one direction, he will discover some new item that reestablishes that perfect balance. The obsessive-compulsive person, in other words, shrinks from the act of decision. It is not surprising that he should. To a person driven by a sense of pressure and guided by moral directives, to a rigid soldier devoted only to duty and cut off from his own wants, the act of decision, which, by its nature, pivots around wants and normally brings with it a sense of freedom and free choice, can only be extremely discomforting. Yet no one can avoid decision, and it is interesting to see the mental operations that appear in obsessive-compulsive people at such times and, as it were, carry them through these occasions.

When he is confronted by the necessity for a decision, even one which may be trivial from a normal standpoint, the obsessive-compulsive person will typically attempt to reach a solution by invoking some rule, principle, or external requirement which might, with some degree of plausibility, provide a "right" answer. He will, in other words, seek some means by which the process of decision-making can be fit into his regular mode of functioning. If he can find some principle or external requirement which plausibly applies to the situation at hand, the necessity for a decision disappears as such; that is, it becomes transformed into the purely technical problem of applying the correct principle. Thus, if he can remember that it is always sensible to go to the cheapest movie, or "logical" to go to the

closest, or good to go to the most educational, the problem re-
solves to a technical one, simply finding which *is* the most educational, the closest, or such. In an effort to find such requirements and principles, he will invoke morality, "logic," social
custom and propriety, the rules of "normal" behavior (especially if he is a psychiatric patient), and so on. In short he will
try to figure out what he "should" do. Sometimes, with one or
more principles in mind, he may add up pros and cons—the advantages to the children on the one side, but the expense on the
other, and so on—hoping that the result of this more complicated technical procedure will be decisive. Sometimes it is, or
rather, may appear to be, and many such "decisions" are a part
of the obsessive-compulsive's daily life. Thus, he decides to wear
one suit rather than another because it is more "appropriate."
But many decisions, particularly those outside his already accustomed routine, are not easily susceptible to being dealt with in
this way. No plausible principle appears, or a number appear,
but none of them sufficiently authoritative. And this is almost
as likely to happen in matters where the objective consequences
are trivial as where they are not.

When the obsessive-compulsive person is unable to reach a
decision by formula or rule, he may begin to stew. He will *struggle* to find the *right* solution. He will tax himself, work at it
night and day, drive himself to "think" about it. But the
obsessive-compulsive person's stewing has very little in common
with the normal person's thinking over of the relevant facts. In
the course of his stewing, the obsessive person will continue long
after he has worn out the relevant facts, and exhausted any possibility of new understanding from them. He will have com-
bined them in all their possible combinations, and done so
many times. He has, in other words, tried once again to deal
with the problem of decision according to his style. He tries to
deal with it as if it were the most taxing technical problem—the
search for the "right" answer. But most of the time this search is
bound to fail. There is no "right" answer in his sense, in the

sense that there is a right answer to a technical problem. The decision, as much as he shrinks from the fact, comes to a choice, a preference.

It is often noticeable that, despite all the hesitation and weighing of pros and cons that precedes the obsessive-compulsive's decision, the actual decision or the actual change will be made exceedingly abruptly. Despite the total length of time consumed, the decision itself will be quite attenuated as compared with the normal person's; it will be very much like a leap. He will finally say or feel something like, "What the hell!" or, "I've got to do something!" and pick the next suit that the salesman happens to offer or quickly sign the contract. Once the choice is made, then, these people will often regard it as a new directive, admitting no new evidence and preferring to feel that the situation no longer allows of modification. Once the obsessive-compulsive can experience this, he can again devote himself with relief to the narrower and more accustomed task of executing the directive. Will power and the general mode of driven activity once again find application. But the interplay between decision and the new data that continuously become available in the course of action, which is central to the activity of a more flexible person, hardly exists for the obsessive-compulsive.

The Loss of Reality

Sometimes obsessive-compulsive people worry (that is, do their taxing mental work) about things that are not merely unlikely but truly absurd. Their worries—hypochondriacal ideas, for example—can be so outlandish that they seem to border on the delusional. Even if one makes allowances for all the motives the obsessional person may have for worry, when he talks as if he believes he has contracted some serious disease through the most remote chain of contacts is this not at least an incipient delusion? Or, for that matter, when such a person has just finished meticulously cleaning a table and acts now as though he believes that the table has instantly again become dirty and requires cleaning, should this be considered delusion? To answer these questions, the fact that he behaves merely "as though" he believes must be considered carefully, for it turns out that the obsessional person does not really believe these things at all. He does not really believe that the table is dirty or that he has been dangerously contaminated in the sense in which we ordinarily use the word "believe." In fact, close examination shows that he never even states that he believes these things to be true. He never says, "I have cancer," or "I have been contaminated." He says, rather, that he might have been contaminated or that he could have cancer, and this is an important difference.

It may be noted, furthermore, that the obsessive-compulsive's interest at such times is different from what we might consider as normal concern. Typically, his greatest interest is in what are essentially "technical details." He tells us with great concern, for example, that such and such a person might have touched such and such a person who, in turn, probably had contact with a doorknob that he has used—details that by their nature are incapable of decisively settling the important matter with which he is ostensibly concerned. These technical details seem to replace matters of substantial truth in his interest. The same issue comes up in connection with obsessional doubt in general. We see that obsessional people have doubts about obvious matters, in circumstances where lack of information, which may give rise to normal doubt, cannot possibly be held accountable. If one assumes that the sense of truth and the meaning of doubt are for the obsessive-compulsive what they are from the normal point of view, one would frequently be forced to the conclusion that the obsessional person is deluded. However, this assumption does not seem to be warranted.

I have described before the narrowing of the obsessive-compulsive's attention, his preoccupation with technical detail, and his missing the flavor or impact of things. This kind of cognition—perhaps together with the general shrinking and restriction of subjective experience of any immediacy—seems to have, with regard to his apprehension of the external world, one additional outstanding consequence: the loss of the experience of conviction.

When one observes obsessive-compulsive people closely or examines their ideas or statements, it becomes clear that such a question as "Does it feel true?" or "Is it really so?" is typically answered neither one way nor the other, but is avoided. Even regarding matters about which he entertains no active doubt, the obsessive-compulsive person will often seem surprised by such a question and virtually dismiss it as irrelevant to his interest. He will not say, "It is true," but will say something like, "It must be" or "It fits."

One compulsive patient, for example, said of the girl he planned to marry, "I must be in love with her—she has all the qualities I want in a wife."

Thus, preoccupation with technical details takes the place of recognition of and response to the actual person or event. The obsessive-compulsive's experience can be compared in this way to the experience of a pilot who flies at night or in a fog with accurate and well-functioning instruments. He can fly his plane, he can fly *as if* he were seeing clearly, but nothing in his situation is experienced directly; only indicators are experienced, things that signify other things.

The same point is illustrated by the case of a lawyer who selected his clothes each morning with the aid of a color wheel. He apparently did not experience the thought or feeling, "This looks good" or "This is nice," but rather, "This fits—according to the rules, it must look good."

A sense of conviction about the world—a sense of truth, in other words—involves a breadth of attention, an interest in and sensitivity to the shadings and proportions of things, and a capacity for direct response to them for which the obsessive-compulsive person is not geared. Instead, he concerns himself with technical details, indicators, which he interprets according to authoritative rules and principles. Consequently, he does not say, "It is," but says instead, "It fits."

A paradox appears at this point in the symptomatology of the obsessive-compulsive. As far as conviction is concerned, he is characterized symptomatically by two outstanding features: doubt and uncertainty, on the one hand, and dogma, on the other. Psychoanalysis has already dissolved this paradox by demonstrating a significant relationship between the two. Dogma arises in order to overcome doubt and ambivalence and to compensate for them. This is a dynamic explanation of the relationship between the two. In addition, I would like to suggest the existence of a formal relationship.

An essential similarity between dogma and obsessional doubt becomes apparent if one asks what feature of the normal person's attitude toward matters of fact is conspicuously absent in both of these. It is that feature I have suggested, that is absent generally from the obsessive-compulsive's experience—a sense of conviction and the whole dimension of interest in real truth. One may go further. Both doubt and dogma rely in an essential way on the narrowed attention and the technical-indicator style of thinking and apprehension of the world characteristic of the obsessive-compulsive. In the case of dogma, this is more obvious. The narrow, rigid attention of the obsessive-compulsive allows him to avoid new information; he regards it not as potentially interesting, but only as potentially distracting. At the same time, his narrow interest in technical indicators allows the dogmatic person to feel completely satisfied with his solutions or, rather, completely satisfied so easily. As long as certain technical requirements are satisfied, his ideas "must be" correct, and he is capable of ignoring their rough edges or even of ignoring facts

that, to another observer, flagrantly and obviously contradict
them. This is the basis of the dogmatic person's and, in general,
the obsessive-compulsive's familiar capacity to produce "logical"
absurdities. But this same narrow interest in technical signs and
indicators also allows the obsessional person to doubt. What
may be, for the normal person, an insignificant detail in relation
to the whole will often be, for the obsessive-compulsive person,
sufficient reason to radically change his perception of the whole.

In other words, the obsessive-compulsive's narrow interest in
technical signs and indicators prevents him from seeing things
in their real proportions, apprehending the rich shadings, or recognizing the real substance of the world and, therefore, makes
him liable both to be satisfied too easily and to doubt too readily. But, if one says that both dogma and doubt ultimately rest
on the obsessive-compulsive's general loss of the experience of
conviction, one may add that, in their extreme forms, they extend that loss and provide additional guarantees against such an
experience. In other words, this viewpoint suggests an additional
dynamic relationship. Both dogma and doubt may be defenses
against the more direct and spontaneous experience of conviction.

I would like to mention one other symptomatic expression of
this mode of thinking and the loss of a sense of truth—the compulsive's great interest in ritual. Ritualistic *behavior* conforms in
a very clear way to the description of obsessive-compulsive activity as mechanical, effortful, and as though in the service of an
external directive. Ritualistic *interest* depends on a narrowly focused, indicator style of cognition and impairment of the sense
of substantial reality. The ritualistic act, as such, must ultimately
seem absurd to one whose sense of reality and interest in truth
are not impaired, no matter how appropriate the symbolic significance of its content may be. It would be no less pointless, as
an act, to the obsessive-compulsive, regardless of the dynamic
forces that may motivate him, if his sense of reality were not
impaired. But all things tend to be, to a greater or lesser degree,

indicators or technical signs for him; his life and interests consist in good part in the apprehension and manipulation of such indicators and signs. The discrepancy, therefore, between symptomatic ritual and apparently nonritualistic obsessive-compulsive behavior is often not as great as it at first seems. Unless this general form of thinking and experience is understood, the ritualistic interest of the obsessive-compulsive person, among all those for whom dynamic issues are not so expressed, cannot be understood.

Paranoid Style

The paranoid style is intrinsically more severely pathological than the other styles considered in this book. It is the only one that, in its more pervasive and extreme forms, involves a psychotic loss of reality. In other respects, also, it generally involves especially severe impairment of normal functioning. However, it would be a mistake to assume that paranoid conditions are invariably psychotic or near psychotic. Characteristically, paranoid modes of functioning, ways of thinking, types of affective experience, and the like, even such specific mental operations as projection, appear in many degrees of severity and, also, are modulated in a great many ways by other factors and tendencies. Aside from the dimension of severity, there are, descriptively and quite roughly speaking, two sorts of people who fall within the category of this style: furtive, constricted, apprehensively suspicious individuals and rigidly arrogant, more aggressively suspicious, megalomanic ones. Of course, since these are only two differentiations of a more general style, they are by no means sharply distinguishable. One can find representatives of a range of severity from frankly delusional states to, perhaps, moderately severe character distortions in both categories.

I cannot attempt to discuss the whole area of specific paranoid manifestations, and I have given rather short shrift even to such general aspects of the style as some of its megalomanic aspects. I have also omitted from the discussion various psychiatric features that are more or less specific to paranoid schizophrenia, such as the varieties of paranoid schizophrenic delusional content. This chapter will deal primarily with those paranoid conditions sometimes described as "paranoid characters." These are essentially nonpsychotic people, although frequently with borderline psychotic features, in whom such paranoid traits as suspiciousness are both pervasive and longstanding. My experience has been chiefly with these people rather than with paranoid schizophrenics, and it seems likely, in any case, that most aspects of the style are more easily examined where there are no schizophrenic complications. Nevertheless, I believe that the general conclusions concerning this style will essentially apply to psychotic paranoid cases as well as to nonpsychotic or borderline ones.

Formal Qualities of Suspicious Thinking and Cognition

When we describe a person as "suspicious," we usually refer to certain ideas, preoccupations, or unwarranted apprehensions of his, such as a continual expectation of trickery. In other words, we usually refer primarily to *what* he thinks, to the contents of his mind, which are, technically speaking, projective contents. But "suspiciousness," especially when it is not merely occasional, but chronic and habitual, also describes a *mode* of thinking and cognition. It implies certain general ways of thinking and modes of attention whose formal qualities can be described independently of their usual contents. For example, it is obvious that suspicious thinking is in some respects unrealistic thinking. Yet, when one considers it, suspicious thinking is unrealistic only in some ways while, in others, it may be sharply perceptive. I mention this example only to suggest what the material of such a formal analysis may consist of and to suggest, also, that such an analysis can disclose some interesting things both about paranoid cognition and paranoid functioning in general.

A formal analysis also presents a view different from our usual one in another respect. Insofar as we are accustomed to regard suspiciousness as a trait or an attitude, I believe that we are inclined to regard it only dynamically, that is, as a consequence of and as explained by a certain affective state. A formal view of suspiciousness, on the other hand, insofar as it discloses stable cognitive modes involved in it, inevitably suggests that these must also have independent sources in the psychological makeup and cognitive development of the paranoid person and that suspiciousness cannot, therefore, be regarded as altogether explained by an affective state. However, this matter need not concern us any further here.

The first formal feature of suspicious thinking that I would like to consider here is, perhaps, also the most fundamental one. Suspicious thinking is thinking that is remarkably and impressively rigid. Let me explain what I mean by this.

A suspicious person is a person who has something on his mind. He looks at the world with fixed and preoccupying expectation, and he searches repetitively, and only, for confirmation of it. He will not be persuaded to abandon his suspicion or some plan of action based on it. On the contrary, he will pay no attention to rational arguments except to find in them some aspect or feature that actually confirms his original view. Anyone who tries to influence or persuade a suspicious person will not only fail, but also, unless he is sensible enough to abandon his efforts early, will, himself, become an object of the original suspicious idea.

Consider the following exchange between a young, quite paranoid patient and his counselor at a psychiatric sanatorium. The patient had planned to move to another city, but, after some delay, he had been notified by the therapist there, Dr. R., that certain essential accommodations would not be available. But the patient had already begun to suspect opposition to his plan on account of the delay.

P: . . . I don't care if nobody wants me to go. I'm still going.
C: But that isn't the point. Dr. R. didn't write that he didn't *want* you to go. He wrote that there's no place there for you to stay.
P: You're trying to talk me out of it, too!
C: I was only saying that, apparently, the way things have turned out, you'll have no decent place to stay.
P: Sure! I knew it! You're just trying to stop me, too! Well, don't try. I'm going! I'm not going to be trapped here!

If one considers the cognitive and attention processes in this exchange, certain things become apparent. This man does not pay attention to the new facts that are, logically speaking, highly relevant to his plans. It is important to note that he does not reject them or deny them. He simply does not pay any attention to them. To be more exact, he does not pay attention to them in the usual way. He sees through them. That is, he does not pay attention to the *apparent* facts, but, instead, he pays sharp attention to any aspect or feature of them or their presentation that lends confirmation to his original suspicious idea.

Suspicious people, in general, do not ignore a piece of data; on the contrary, they examine it quite carefully. But they examine it with an extraordinary prejudice, dismissing what is not relevant to their suppositions and seizing on anything that confirms them. The fact is, furthermore, that their dismissal and disregard of anything that does not confirm their prior supposition is an active and intentional process. They do this on principle, since they operate from the outset on the assumption that anything that does not confirm their expectation is "mere appearance." Thus, they would say that they are interested in penetrating the sham, the pretense, and the superficial; they want to get at the heart of the matter, the underlying truth. But this need not prevent us from noticing that the underlying truth invariably turns out to be precisely what they expected it to be in the first place.

I would like to examine this suspicious mode of cognition and thinking further and to attempt to analyze some of its components. I will try to show that it is characterized by an extremely tense and rigid *directedness* of attention, akin to what I have described in connection with obsessive-compulsive attention; but it is far more severe. From this quality of rigid directedness of attention, both the glaring failures of paranoid cognition and its occasional brilliant successes follow.

Suspicious people are not simply people who are apprehensive and "imagine things." They are, in actual fact, extremely keen and often penetrating observers. They not only imagine, but also search. And they not only search, but also search with an intensity of attention and an acuteness that may easily surpass the capacity of normal attention. Psychologists are familiar, for example, with the capacity of these people to detect the most subtle asymmetry on a Rorschach inkblot or some tiny feature of a TAT card that has previously escaped the notice even of an experienced tester who thinks he knows the card "by heart." The attention of these people is, furthermore, not only unusually acute and intense, but also unusually active. It is not the careful studying and measuring attention of the obsessive-compulsive, but an actively scanning and searching attention. Anyone who has come under the scrutiny of a paranoid and suspicious person is familiar with this quality. Nothing out of the ordinary will escape his attention and, certainly, nothing that is even remotely related to his concerns or his preoccupations of the moment.

One such patient, fearful of hypnosis when he first came to a therapist's office, inquired about a book on hypnotherapy that he had "just happened to notice" on a crowded bookshelf about twelve feet away!

What is the significance of this kind of attention? Is it, after all, so remarkable? If we were to speak for the paranoid person, we might say that this extraordinary intensity of attention is only a response to extraordinary circumstances, namely, an external threat or danger, and that anyone would respond to such danger with vigilance. But the fact is, in the first place, that, even if we grant him his premise of an external danger, it is not quite true that anyone would respond in the same way. Hysterical people, for example, seem to respond to external danger in just the opposite cognitive direction, by a fuzzing of attention; they do not search for the external threat, but shrink from it. In the second place, this intensity and acuteness of attention is not merely occasionally or sporadically characteristic of paranoid people, but is continuous. In fact, approximately the same intensity of attention that characterizes them when they scrutinize a stranger characterizes them, also, when they apply themselves to an arithmetic problem or a problem of abstraction on an intelligence test (where, incidentally, it often contributes to a superior score). This kind of attention, in other words, represents an authentic cognitive mode. These people are not merely capable of remarkably active, intense, and searching attention; they seem essentially incapable of anything else. They are always sharp-eyed and searching, always intensely concentrating. Their attention is never passive or casual, never simply wandering. These are the characteristics I mean to describe by saying that suspicious attention is continuously, rigidly, and tensely directed attention. It is attention that always has an aim, is always purposeful, searching *for* something. To put it another way, it is attention that is rigidly intentional.

This kind of cognition has certain further interesting and important correlates. Attention that is so rigidly directed, so intensely searching for something, must become, in the extreme case, biased attention. Let me explain what I mean by this. Most people observe the world with some preconceptions, convictions, and ideas that guide their observations, and, in turn, these conceptions are influenced and modified by what they see, particularly, by what they see that they did not expect to see.

Other people—we usually call them "suggestible"—look at the world with much less in the way of firm conviction or point of view, and they are easily impressed by whatever vivid fact or loud opinion currently happens along their path. Still other people regard the world with such rigid directedness, such definite interest and point of view, that they are never led by facts, but, on the contrary, they impose their own anticipations on whatever facts they encounter.

On the one hand, the paranoid person searches intensely for confirmation of his anticipations. On the other hand, those same rigid anticipations of what he will find allow him to feel entitled to discredit and disregard apparent contradiction. Between these two attitudes, he is bound to "find" what he is looking for. In this process, intellectual capacity, keenness, and acuteness of attention become not guarantees of realistic judgment, but, on the contrary, instruments of bias. This keenness enables suspicious people to make, as they often do, brilliantly perceptive mistakes. Acuteness and intensity of attention, when it is this rigid, becomes exceedingly narrow in its focus; and the ultimate object of the suspicious person's intense, narrowly focused, and biased search is what we commonly call a "clue." The clue is the confirming evidence, perhaps insignificant to anyone else, that the suspicious person seizes on while at the same time disregarding all modifying and corrective facts that may surround it.

A patient felt that his boss "wanted to make him jump through the hoop," and he would have none of it. The patient had a good deal of evidence to prove his point, all of it probably quite factual and some of it quite keenly observed. Yet, to someone else, even these facts did not add up to a particularly unusual boss. True, the boss had insisted that the work be done his way and not the patient's way. He did make a point of promptness, perhaps unnecessarily. He had objected to the patient's apparently cool manner with certain of the customers. And, quite possibly, he had even done all of this with a certain edge in his voice or the look of a man who didn't mind the opportunity of bringing an independent young fellow to heel. All these items may have been there, as most of them often are in bosses, because they include a good deal of what bosses are supposed to accomplish. To the patient, however, they were unmistakable clues to the man's real motives: to make him crawl and to emasculate him. Who knows? Perhaps even this motive was not altogether absent. But all these clues appeared in a context that the patient disregarded but that radically alters the significance of them and, for that matter, that even modulates the starkness of the motives imputed to the man. The fact is, there was work to be done, and the boss was responsible for it; and the difference between a boss who pursues this objective too aggressively and a man whose principal interest is to cut down his subordinate is a very great difference indeed.

Acute, narrow attention that is rigidly directed toward certain evidence can extract it and can impose its own conclusions virtually anywhere. Thus, the suspicious person can be at the same time absolutely right in his perception and absolutely wrong in his judgment. This is bias—in a sense the psychological opposite of suggestibility. This kind of cognition has many manifestations in paranoid symptoms. It is evident not only in suspiciousness, but also is a cognitive base of paranoid dogma and is manifest in the manner of confirmation and development of megalomanic theories and ideas. This mode of cognition is, in fact, one basis for the particular nature of the paranoid loss of reality, and, as I will try to show later, it cannot account for certain of the special and peculiar features of paranoid psychotic thinking and projective ideas.

There is another formal characteristic of suspicious cognition that requires mention here, a characteristic that gives a special slant and adds a special qualification to the more general picture of rigidity and intensity. Suspicious people are also conspicuously hypersensitive and hyperalert. These people are exceedingly, nervously sensitive to anything out of the ordinary or unexpected; any such item, however trivial or slight it might seem from the standpoint of the normal person, will trigger their attention in its full, searching intensity. It is not simply that suspi-

cious people are easily startled, for instance, by a noise outside
the door. More than that, the source of that start immediately
becomes a fresh object of suspicious scrutiny, at the least, of a
quick but sharp-eyed search. This hyperalertness is, in other
words, not simply a frightened response or a nervous one; it is
something more than that. These people seem to want to cover
everything, and any new element will also need to be examined
according to the dimensions of their suspicious interest and concern.

The fact is that the unexpected, the surprising, the unusual,
or even the new is no friend to any rigid person—neither to the
suspicious person nor even to the simply dogmatic one. To a
rigid person, the unusual or unexpected is threatening simply
because it *is* unusual or unexpected, aside from whatever else it
may be. No such person can afford or tolerate the attitude of
uncertainty, not to speak of open-mindedness or receptivity,
which the unexpected or unusual, in a sense, demands and
which, in the normal person, it receives. The rigid or dogmatic
compulsive simply ignores the unusual; he narrowly follows his
own line of thought and goes right by anything out of the way.
The paranoid person, however—and we shall consider why later
—cannot do this. Instead, he avoids surprise by virtually anticipating it. The paranoid quality that we describe as "hyperalertness" consists of exactly this, and it is this activeness that distinguishes hyperalertness from a merely frightened or startled
response. The suspicious person is ready for anything unexpected and immediately becomes aware of it. And he does not
merely become aware of the unexpected, but must then bring
his full attention to bear on it. He must scrutinize it, cover it, or,
as it were, get on top of it. He must, in other words, bring it into
the orbit of his scheme of things and, in effect, satisfy himself
that it is not or at least is no longer surprising.

This does not mean, it is important to note, that the suspicious person must satisfy himself that the unusual event—the
noise outside the door, the canceled appointment, the letter

that comes unexpectedly late or unexpectedly early—is innocent. On the contrary, he may very well conclude that it is far
from innocent and still feel satisfied. But what he cannot tolerate is the existence of the unusual without scrutiny, that is, its
existence in a form that can still surprise him. Indeed, we may
draw an interesting conclusion from the nature of this hyperalertness: It is not a concrete danger, but surprise, that the suspicious person dreads most.

How does this alter the general picture of suspicious cognition? I believe that it must be concluded that this cognition is
characterized not only by rigid directedness of attention, but
also by directedness that is maintained in a state of such extreme
tension that it resembles a muscle so tense it springs to the
touch. This is not merely a greater quantity of the normal kind
of alertness; and it is not merely the alertness of a well-trained
soldier or an expert hunter. It is much closer to the alertness of a
soldier or hunter who has begun to tire, experiences increased
subjective tension, and, without realizing it, begins to press himself harder. This is the soldier, one imagines, who is likely to
shoot at shadows. The paranoid condition of hyperalertness, in
other words, seems to reflect a rigidity of attention that contains
some underlying weakness or instability and, consequently, is
not only maintained in a state of extreme tension, but also is
easily triggered.

It is not difficult to imagine, in a very general way, the development of a cognitive mode such as the one I have described,
even without being in a position to identify all its sources. I
have suggested that the intellectual rigidity of the obsessive-
compulsive may be regarded as a distortion, in the direction of
hypertrophy, of the normal cognitive development of the capacity for directedness of attention—the capacity to direct, focus, and sustain attention at will, purposefully or intentionally.
Normally, from this development such adult cognitive capacities
must arise as the capacity to concentrate, to sustain and pursue a
line of thought, to penetrate the immediately obvious in order

to focus sharply on what is relevant to one's own interests, and
the like. From this point of view, the form of paranoid suspicious cognition appears as an even more extreme distortion of
this aspect of normal cognitive development, a distortion that
involves a more severely rigid, exceedingly tense, and apparently
not altogether stable hypertrophy of many features of its normal
outcome.

The Paranoid Loss of Reality

No one would deny that the suspicious person distorts reality
or that he suffers a serious impairment of reality experience, but
the exact nature of that impairment is less evident. For instance,
it is not blanket impairment, but impairment of certain classes
of reality experience that characterizes these people. Although
we are certainly entitled to speak of severe distortion of reality,
we know that it must be distortion of a quite special kind, since,
even in its most severe forms, it seems to regularly allow certain
kinds of congruence with normal reality experience. I would like
to try to clarify the nature of this impairment and distortion and
to show that it can account for certain features of the paranoid
person's subjective world.

Let us consider a question. What aspects of the world is the
suspicious person, the person who is never able to relax his sharp-
eyed scrutiny and take a casual look around, most likely to miss?
Let me offer a tentative and partial answer. He will miss precisely what, to the normal person, would be the obvious, the
apparent, the plain face value of things. Suspicious people disdain the obvious; they say, in effect, that it is only misleading,
superficial, not the real essence of the matter, but something to
be seen through.

Thus, after some time in psychotherapy, a suspicious patient
conceded, perhaps overstating the point, that he never actually
listened to what the therapist said; he listened, rather, for signs *in*
what was said of what the therapist "really thought."

This patient heard everything that another person might hear; in fact, he probably missed a good deal less of what was said in his presence than the normal person would. But this is not a matter of hearing; it is a matter of listening. It is a matter, in other words, of the direction and mode of interest and attention. The sound technician may listen to a recording very attentively, and he may hear far more than the average person, but he cannot, at the same time, listen to the music. The patient in the above example, like suspicious people generally, listened and watched very sharply, but he listened for something quite different from the normal object of interest. He listened and watched only for clues to what, according to his suppositions, the therapist might be up to. He probably noticed every unusual phrase or flicker of hesitation. But, meanwhile, the whole sense of the communication, its otherwise apparent point and substance, its face value, was correspondingly diminished for him. The suspicious person, in other words, regards a communication or a situation not to apprehend what it is, but to understand what it signifies. Like the obsessive-compulsive, the paranoid looks at the world for indicators and constructs a subjective world from them. But the indicators that interest the paranoid person, his clues, are much narrower ones and are tied to specific biases or suspicious suppositions. His loss of the world as it apparently is, consequently, is much greater than that which the compulsive person sustains on account of his preoccupation with technical data.

When a person loses interest in and a sense of the plain, apparent world in favor only of narrowly perceived indicators, clues, or signs of this or that, he not only loses a sense of that which gives the world its tone and color, but also loses a sense of that which would normally modify and qualify the significance of the indicators themselves; he loses a sense of proportion. For instance, fanatical people (among whom, incidentally, the paranoid style is usually well represented), such as fanatical antivivisectionists, may see signs of human cruelty not only in the beat-

ing of a horse, but also in a scientific experiment. They may
have a point. The sign may really be there. But it is not *all* that
is there. Such a loss of proportion occurs in suspicious people in
extreme forms.

It is useful, therefore, to regard the paranoid person's construction of a subjective world as having two aspects: on the one
hand, a biased seizing of "significant" clues from their context
and, on the other hand, a loss of appreciation of that context,
which is just what normally gives the small clue item its actual
significance. These two aspects, the negative as well as the posi-
tive, both figure in every piece of suspicious distortion of reality.
Thus, when the patient cited earlier picks out some nuance of
his boss' latest order as confirmation of his idea that the boss
wants to degrade him and when, at the same time, he is oblivious to the whole, normally apparent context of that order,
namely, the responsibility of the boss simply to get work done,
then, whatever else is involved, the normal everyday cognitive
functions of judgment and sense of proportion have failed.

In this way, a subjective world can be constructed in which
facts, accurately enough perceived in themselves, are endowed
with a special interpretive significance in place of their actual
significance. A subjective world comes into being that is a peculiar blend of the autistic and the factual. The paranoid person's
picture of the world is interpretively autistic, but it is usually
accurate in its factual details. He imposes a biased and autistic
interpretive scheme on the factual world. His interest is not in
the apparent world, but in the world behind the apparent world
to which the apparent world only gives clues. Thus, the subject
matter of his interest has to do with hidden motives, underlying
purposes, special meanings, and the like. He does not necessarily
disagree with the normal person about the existence of any
given fact; he disagrees only about its significance.

This fact has certain interesting consequences. For example, it
makes it possible for even severely paranoid people to recognize
various essential facts of the normal social world sufficiently to

achieve a limited adjustment to it, even though they may privately interpret substantial portions of that world autistically. Thus, such a person may perfectly well recognize the necessity of paying his taxes, but, at the same time, he may regard their collection as part of some fantastic government scheme. He may even recognize that it is prudent to keep his unusual ideas to himself. It becomes possible in this way for these people to live, subjectively, in the world of apparent reality as one might live in a foreign country, with people who, in their ignorance, do not see things clearly and are not even hospitable to those who do but with whom it is nevertheless both necessary and perfectly possible to deal. Perhaps paranoid cases of so-called "encapsulated" delusions are actually of this sort, involving not merely limited areas of delusional content, but also types of content that, since they deal only with the significance of apparent reality, do not necessarily flagrantly violate the facts of apparent reality and so permit the delusional person to live in both worlds at the same time.

Distortion of reality of this sort may be quite far advanced—involving a severe loss of a sense of the real and substantial world in favor of autistic interpretive preoccupations—without the impairment of logical processes that one finds in schizophrenia. Probably, this phenomenon is responsible for the fact that certain severely paranoid persons, if they are also close-mouthed, are difficult to distinguish from constricted or inhibited normals, even on the Rorschach test.[1] It is probably responsible, also, for the curious quality that some delusional paranoid constructions have of seeming almost certainly autistic but just conceivably true. Since these constructions may be woven fairly logically from autistic interpretations of actual facts, such as recent newspaper items, they can sometimes be quite uncomfortably convincing.

---

[1] See Roy Schafer, *Clinical Interpretation of Psychological Tests* (New York: International Universities Press, 1948).

In general, since one can imagine almost any degree of purely interpretive distortion of reality—any degree, in other words, of loss of the world of apparent reality in favor of a world constructed of clues, without the necessity of any destruction of logical thought processes—it becomes possible to conceive of a continuous range of paranoid conditions from quite nonpsychotic to severely psychotic ones. This range would begin, perhaps, with mildly suspicious attitudes and reach an extreme point not in schizophrenia, but in utterly rigid, perhaps logically elaborated or "systematized" delusions that still consist of interpretations built around certain accurately perceived clues—the so-called "kernels of reality" in paranoid delusions—wrenched from their real context. Such cases of "pure" paranoia must be rare, however, although, apparently, they do exist. In practice, one almost always finds that psychotic paranoid conditions involve schizophrenic elements as well, and, therefore, the actual extreme point in the range of paranoid conditions is generally a form of schizophrenia that, however, still shows relatively less thought disorganization than any other form of schizophrenia.

PROJECTION: COGNITIVE ASPECTS

We come here to what must be more familiar psychiatric territory, but let me start with a definition. "Projection," in the sense with which we are concerned here, means the attribution to external figures of motivations, drives, or other tensions that are repudiated and intolerable in oneself. This mental operation or mechanism is so central to our understanding of paranoid pathology and symptoms that it has almost come to define what is called "paranoid" in psychiatry. Yet, the process of projection, as distinct from its evident results, is not well understood. The question remains, why should this mechanism be so particularly associated with this type of person? This mechanism and, therefore, this problem has cognitive aspects, but it obviously also has noncognitive ones. Here, we will restrict ourselves to the former, and we will turn to the latter further on.

It is true, of course, that projection occurs in nonparanoid as well as paranoid people, and it is true, furthermore, that, in a more general sense, the tendency to impose internal tensions on the perceived external world is universal. One example is the universal tendency to understand natural events animistically, but there are many other more homely examples. Perhaps, any kind of empathic error or distortion—the way people often "understand" their pets, for instance—can be regarded as a reflection of this tendency. Possibly, one could also include the tendency of the person in love to endow the object of that love with undeserved characteristics or the tendency of people who feel frightened or small to endow their enemies with greater size or more power than is actually warranted. Indeed, the very fact that people organize the world subjectively—see it in their own way and according to the dimensions of their own interests—the fact that people are imaginative and interpretive, and, most particularly, the fact that they are empathic in their understanding of the world opens a great variety of "projective" possibilities and tends to reduce the apparent uniqueness of projective phenomena. Nevertheless, it remains true that, in the more specific sense, projection is primarily a fact of paranoid functioning, and the existence of various universal projective tendencies cannot explain why. Nor can an understanding of certain general defensive advantages that projection seems to provide. For example, it may be said that projection accomplishes an advantageous transformation of such an internal threat as that created by the pressure of an intolerable impulse into a more manageable external threat. But the very fact that such a transformation, on the face of it, seems to be so generally advantageous only raises the question again: Why should this process be so particularly characteristic of some people, whereas it is hardly characteristic at all of others?

I suggest that the general cognitive mode we have been discussing and, particularly, the special sort of loss of reality intrinsic to that mode comprises a basis for the cognitive aspects of projection. I am not saying that such a cognitive mode *is* projection; it is not. It is not even a sufficient condition for regular and pervasive projection, but it is a necessary one.

What cognitive processes are involved in projection? Most conspicuously, every projection involves a distortion of reality. But it involves a distortion of reality of a special form. Thus, projection does *not* involve blanket denials of reality or blanket exclusions of portions or segments of reality in favor of autistic constructions; it does not involve amnesia, memory loss, or a fuzzy romanticizing of reality; it does not involve autistic constructions flatly and arbitrarily "pasted" over reality; it does not typically involve hallucinatory experiences, at least until the process is severely complicated by schizophrenic elements. All these are reality distortions, true enough, but they are not what we mean by projection and, in certain ways, are, in fact, quite fundamentally different from it.

Projection, unlike these other sorts of reality impairment, does not involve a breakdown of cognition and a withdrawal of attention from the external world. On the contrary, it occurs in the act of cognition and with keen attention to the external world. Thus, projection is generally faithful to and does not distort apparent reality, nor does it usually include perceptual distortion. Projection distorts the significance of apparent reality; it is an autistic interpretive distortion of external reality. This is why the subject matter of projection does not usually deal with the apparent and the actual, but with the potential and the hidden, with the intentions of others, their motives, thoughts, feelings, and the like. Projection invariably consists of an interpretively biased cognition of actual events or behavior. This is its cognitive form, and this, although not necessarily this alone, distinguishes it from such other failures of reality apprehension as perceptual distortion or hallucination. The projective process is completed and a projection may be said to exist when the paranoid person, in a certain state of tension and biased expectancy vis-à-vis the external world, turns his attention toward an object and seizes on a clue the significance of which convinces him of some motive, intention, or the like, and thereby crystallizes his biased expectancy in some concrete shape.

For example, such simple and even seemingly perceptual projections as, "He is watching me disapprovingly," or, "He thinks I'm a queer," actually consist of autistically biased, quasi-empathic, interpretive cognitions of that person's glance, his look, an ambiguous phrase, or other small piece of behavior.

In more complex projections, such interpretively distorted cognitions may be woven together to support a general projective interpretation. For instance, an extremely paranoid businessman, who imagined that his partners had concocted schemes to do away with him and who had fled his native country, had, according to all indications, correctly discerned their interest in getting him out of the business, actually observed evidence of meetings held without him, noticed strange looks, and the like. His projective ideas consisted of fantastic but, again, quasi-empathic interpretations of these facts woven together.

It is commonly observed that the paranoid person "meets reality halfway" in his projections or that projection is a "compromise with reality." These observations simply express, in a very approximate way, the essential fact that projection actually consists of a cognitive act, albeit one of a special and especially biased, distorted kind. Indeed, these observations have interest only as long as one has in mind a comparison, say, with hallucination; but they become trivial when projection is regarded as a cognition, since meeting reality halfway is, after all, the very least one can expect of cognition. From this standpoint, it is only remarkable that a mode of cognition is possible that allows, and in certain people regularly allows, an interpretive bias and distortion of such proportions as to meet reality *only* halfway and many times, as we know, not even that.

In other words, it is remarkable that a person is able to look at an object in the external world, look at *it* and not somewhere else, not with fuzzy or scattered attention, not with confusion, and not with a withdrawn, blank stare, but squarely, sharply, and clear-eyed, and still pronounce an all but complete unreality. Yet, this is what the paranoid person does in a projection. One can observe it behaviorally, and one can see the evidence of his attentiveness even within the projection itself. It is not that he sees something that is really there, in the act of an attentive cognition, but that he sees so much that is *not* there, in the same cognitive act—that requires explanation.

How is it possible? According to what we can judge from the cognitive form of the projection, it is possible because, when he looks at that object, his attention is actually rigidly, narrowly focused on some feature or aspect of it that is for him a clue, and his mind is on that clue's significance. His interest and attention is drawn to the discovery of that clue in the first place by a biased expectancy, such as a suspicious and apprehensive anticipation, and the clue, once found, is understood according to the same bias. Such expectancy or bias need not itself be conscious, but it determines what is of conscious interest, what next seems important and what does not, and it determines what the subjective significance of the newly discovered clue is.

For instance, a furtive man who has made a small mistake on the job will search his boss' face and words with a certain expectation. He is looking for a sign of dislike, say, or disapproval, although he, himself, is not likely to be aware that he is looking for it. When he finds that sign, the projectively distorted, quasi-empathic cognition is complete, and an uncrystallized bias or expectancy is transformed into a conviction: "He dislikes me."

Thus, the clue and its significance are what the paranoid person sees when he looks at the external object, and he will see that and only that no matter how keenly he looks or how many times. It is also true, of course, that such a cognition may at the same time reveal, in an especially vivid or magnified way, an actual feature or aspect of the external object that coincides with the projective expectancy and is seized on for that reason.

If this understanding of the cognitive form of a projection is correct, then it is, I believe, clear that the general cognitive mode of the paranoid person will facilitate it. To the extent that any cognitive mode is interpretive, to the extent that an individual searches for what he regards as more significant and turns away from what he regards as less significant, bias, including projective bias, is possible and perhaps even inevitable. Normal cognition, however, generally possesses sufficient flexibility to correct that bias. But cognition that is as rigidly and narrowly directed as that of the paranoid, as immune to correction, as capable of ignoring the apparent and searching only for signs in it that confirm its bias, a cognition that brings with it a loss of a sense of proportion and appreciation of the plain face value of things—such cognition is liable to interpretive distortions of the wildest kind, that is, distortions of a projective form.

In projection, internal tension is transformed in some way into tension vis-à-vis the external world, into biased anticipation of the external world, and, finally, into conviction about the external world. These considerations explain only the lesser part of that process, namely, the step from biased anticipation to conviction. This is the cognitive aspect. But the greater part of the process, the transformation of internal tension into external tension and the creation of bias, is another matter and no longer a cognitive one. Indeed, that transformation of tension is quite inseparable from a whole subjective state and general style of functioning that is characteristically paranoid.

The General Paranoid Problem of Autonomy

Paranoid people live in readiness for an emergency. They seem to live in a more or less continuous state of total mobilization. The condition of tension that is manifest in their alertness and their intense, searching attention seems, for example, reflected also in their body musculature. One has only to touch a paranoid person lightly on the shoulder and feel the springing response, itself immediately attenuated or countermanded, to become aware of this. This general condition of mobilization has various clinical forms. Sometimes, it takes a more aggressive form, with edginess and readiness to counterattack; sometimes, it takes the form of extreme carefulness and tense control; and, sometimes, it is well described simply as defensive vigilance.

We are accustomed to thinking of the paranoid person's mobilization, as we are of his specific cognitive alertness, only in terms of its subjective aim: the necessity to cope with (projective) external threat or danger. But, while it has this subjective aim, it also has a form; it is, including its subjective aim, a way of functioning. In a manner of speaking, one should not be too empathic in a formal study. Our interest here is not to understand a piece of behavior from the paranoid person's viewpoint, but to understand a general way of functioning, even including, if possible, the place that viewpoint has in it.

From a formal standpoint, how can we describe this paranoid condition of mobilization more adequately? Let me first try to describe it in general terms. It is a condition of extraordinarily rigid and tense directedness of behavior and of marked intensification of such normal voluntary faculties as attention, muscular control, and, on a different level, purposiveness. It is a psychological condition that can be described as one of "hyperintentionality," a condition that is, in all probability, accompanied by chronic hypertonus of the voluntary musculature. Thus, it is the general condition of which the hyperalert, suspicious mode of cognition is one aspect.

Consider the relationship of the paranoid person to certain areas of his own behavior. I have in mind the kind of behavior that is ordinarily described as expressive behavior, such as gesture, facial expression, tone of voice, manner of sitting, and the like. One can easily notice in such a person that, although he enters the room with a greeting or perhaps a smile, sits down with apparent ease, and even begins to talk with what looks like comfortable familiarity, it all somehow seems like an imitation of the real thing. One realizes that what at first looked like expressive behavior is not really that at all. It is not friendly; it is only designed to look friendly.

Sometimes, this behavior is executed quite smoothly or at least with mechanical evenness, and, in many relatively stable paranoid characters, particularly, one gets the impression that everything, down to the pressure of the handshake, is practiced to a fine point. These people may be prepared, with only a flicker of hesitation, to be or, rather, to act casual, enthusiastic, serious, or whatever else they believe the tactics of the situation call for. We know, in general, what the aim of this behavior is—it is essentially defensive—but consider, also, its mode. In paranoid people, areas of behavior that are normally expressive or spontaneous, automatic, and involuntary and that normally reflect quite thoroughly integrated and automatic sequences of feeling or impulse and manifest behavior are, instead, purposive, intentional, and within the domain of voluntary control. Even the mechanical smoothness of such behavior reflects not flexibility, but only the extensiveness and effectiveness of intentional control.

This is not just to say that the paranoid person lacks spontaneity of behavior or that he watches himself very carefully, curbing any expressiveness so as not to reveal himself. That much is certainly true, and it is particularly evident in those wooden and impassive-looking paranoid individuals—one such patient had long been nicknamed, in his family, "The Stick"—who carefully avoid betraying any expression at all. Schafer[2] has likened this kind of inner surveillance and the suppressive measures that accompany it to an "internal police state." But something more general is also involved. At the same time as one area of functioning—expressiveness or spontaneity of behavior—shrinks radically under this regime, another area—the domain of intention-

[2] Roy Schafer, *Psychoanalytic Rorschach Interpretation* (New York: Grune and Stratton, 1954).

ality or conscious direction of behavior—becomes enlarged. The
paranoid person not only watches and curbs his behavior, but
also, more generally, he controls and steers it; he steers his body,
facial expressions, and gestures like a general deploying troops.

Thus, the directedness of paranoid behavior is just as evident
in the haughty and pointedly disdainful poses of arrogant paranoid characters as it is in the caution of more obviously guarded
ones. And it is perhaps most striking of all among those paranoid people who mechanically assume a pose of spontaneity,
casualness, and a hearty hail-fellow-well-met self-confidence.

One such patient, who always greeted his therapist with an arti-
ficially enthusiastic smile, was regularly observed by a secretary to
turn on the smile some short distance before he actually reached
the therapist's door, while he was still in the empty hall.

It is not only that such specific physical behavior as gesture,
expression, body movement, and the like, is so remarkably directed and intentional. The directedness of this behavior is only
part of a larger directedness, namely, of activity as a whole. I
mean by this that whatever the paranoid person does has an
aim, a purpose. He does not say what he says just because it
strikes him or because he feels like it. He never does anything
whimsically, impulsively, for its immediate appeal, or for its own
sake. What he says and does is designed, intended, and purposeful. (It is interesting to note that he assumes this to be the case
for other people as well.) We observe this fact when we observe
the deviousness of paranoid people, when we notice that what
seemed like an ordinary conversation is, on their side, a tactical
operation and full of jockeying. Their behavior may have a self-
aggrandizing motive, or it may have an evasive or defensive motive, but, in any case, it is designed. They stand behind their
behavior in general as they stand behind their body or facial
expressions, steering, directing, always with intention and never
with abandon.

In this way, normally expressive and spontaneous functions

assume, in the paranoid person, the status of instruments. This cannot help but have certain subjective consequences. Expressive behavioral functions—smiling, talking, doing—which, for the normal person, are simply a part of "him," are, for the paranoid person, not a part of him, but under his direction. The normal person, on the whole, feels his body to be "him," whereas the paranoid person regards his body as his instrument. This suggests another general result of the paranoid mobilization of faculties. When the domain of behavioral functions under intentional direction becomes enlarged at the expense of normal areas of spontaneity and expressiveness, the domain subjectively experienced as "him" tends to contract, ultimately to a tight and compact administrative center.

Spontaneity and expressiveness of behavior is not the only area of freedom that suffers under the rigid paranoid mobilization or "internal police state." Subjective experience itself, particularly including affective experience, is severely restricted and narrowed, and certain classes of affects seem to be all but obliterated. For example, paranoid people rarely laugh. They may act as if they are laughing, but they do not laugh genuinely, that is, they do not seem to feel amused.

Such a loss of affective experience cannot be regarded as a result of inner surveillance or as an intentional act of suppression. The paranoid person may steer and direct his behavior meticulously, but he is no more able than anyone else to make a feeling disappear. While the loss of affective experience is not a result of an intention or a direction, it is a result of the state of rigid directedness and intentionality. In a nation under conditions of emergency mobilization, a great deal of normal life is lost, not only—in fact, not even primarily—by decree. It is also lost because interest in many of the normal activities of life is incompatible with the mood created and the energy and attention demanded by the emergency and the mobilization for it. A similar thing happens in the psychology of the paranoid person. It is impossible to be mobilized as he is—alert, watching himself, rigidly steering every gesture and expression—and at the same time to be amused. And to whatever extent it may be possible momentarily, such a feeling will surely be regarded as subversive. For example, when such patients loosen up somewhat in psychotherapy and do occasionally laugh genuinely, they invariably become acutely uncomfortable, do everything they can to stop it, and feel that such a thing is "ridiculous in a grown man."

In general, those classes of affects that might be described as more passive or soft, such as tender or sentimental feelings, seem to be largely absent in the conscious experience of paranoid people, and this seems equally to be the case in those paranoid individuals who are furtive and constricted as it is for those who are arrogant and megalomanic. Tenderness and sentiment, in other words, are equally incompatible with a general frame of mind that is rigidly tight and guarded and with one that is rigidly haughty and militant. Where tender or sentimental feelings do appear, they are usually considered to be weak or effeminate and are regarded with shame, if they are internal, or with disdain, if they appear in someone else. Not only the range of affects, but also the range of interests, contracts and narrows in these people. Playfulness disappears, and playful interests are usually absent. Paranoid people are usually uninterested in art or aesthetics. Such interests are also likely to be, according to their lights, soft, weak, or effeminate. Finally, there is one other area of narrowed subjective experience that may be added to this list, although I offer it only as an impression that would be difficult to confirm. It is my impression that, under the general paranoid regime of rigid mobilization, there is also a constriction of bodily, sensual experience; for example, sexuality tends to become quite mechanical and diminishes in sensual pleasure.

It is interesting to note, considering the general narrowing of their interests, that paranoid people *are* frequently deeply interested in mechanical things, devices, electrical apparatus, and the like. I mean this without reference to the frequency with which such items appear in paranoid delusional content. Actually, their feeling involves more than mere interest. Paranoid people often seem to have a special respect, perhaps an exorbitant one, for such mechanical things and mechanical schemes as computers, automation schemes, and the like. Indeed, their respect for mechanical and electronic things and methods contrasts sharply with their disdain for a good deal of humanness, particularly, instances of what they regard as soft, weak, or defective humanity, such as sick or weak people, sentimental people, or females. Altogether, one may easily get the impression from their respect for the one and disdain for the other that they would prefer a world that was completely mechanized, in which nature's manifest sloppiness and sentimental tolerances would be eliminated. Such attitudes make it additionally plain that the paranoid person's mobilization, with its rigid, mechanical directedness of behavior, is no alien and regretted emergency measure, but, on the contrary, is a thoroughgoing mode of functioning interwoven with supporting attitudes; and, if it were in the power of many paranoid characters to do so, no doubt the mode would be perfected still further.

There is no need to carry the description of this aspect of the paranoid style any further. Paranoid mobilization implies radical constriction and narrowing of those areas of normal life that are essentially involuntary and virtual elimination of the capacity for abandonment along with the subjection of behavior to rigid directedness. If this describes a form of functioning, what is its significance? I will try to show that this formal mode represents a pathology of autonomy even more severe than that represented by the obsessive-compulsive style, and one that has further consequences, not only a rigid, but also an essentially frail distortion and exaggeration of the normal person's authority over himself. I would also like to make several special points: first, that the nature of the paranoid person's most characteristic concerns, both those that are projectively elaborated and those that are not, are varieties of concern about autonomy and, second, that a defensive and antagonistic relationship to the external world or, at least, to certain features of it, is intrinsic to this mode of functioning, *even before projection.*

In the paranoid person, even more sharply and severely than in the case of the obsessive-compulsive, every aspect and component of normal autonomous functioning appears in rigid, distorted, and, in general, hypertrophied form. Thus, the normal person is capable of directedness of attention, as in volitional concentration or pursuit of a line of thought, but he is also capable of passive attention, as in being impressed by the unexpected; but the paranoid person's attention is so purposefully and narrowly directed as to amount, not merely to rigidity, but to a fixed bias. The normal person is capable of smooth and unself-conscious body control, but he is also capable of body freedom and bodily, sensuous pleasure. The paranoid person is not merely stiff, but directs his body like a general directing troops. While the normal person is capable of purposeful, intentional activity, he is also capable of abandonment. But the paranoid person is totally mobilized; all action is purposeful, directed toward an aim (for example, a defensive aim) with an intensity close to what is normally reserved for emergency. Nothing is done playfully, whimsically, for its own sake, or with abandon. This mode of functioning, pervaded by tension, certainly does not represent a greater degree of the normal person's autonomy. It reflects, rather, an exceedingly frail autonomy, one that, because it is so frail, can be maintained only in this remarkably rigid and exaggerated form. If anyone should doubt this, he need only consider not just the objective, but also certain aspects of the subjective outcome of the normal person's achievement of autonomy and their comparative paranoid forms. Let me explain what I mean.

Volition or intentionality requires the development of equipment—muscular equipment, for example—and the competency to use it. Indeed, one might say that, at the beginning at least, the capacity for volitional or willful behavior—the capacity for being one's own master in this sense—is precisely a matter of competency, for example, the muscular competency involved in holding on or letting go at will. This is not all that is involved in autonomous functioning. Being one's own master means being and feeling *free* to do what one wants to do as well as being *able*, that is, competent, to do what one wants to do. But competency is always an aspect of autonomy, new competencies probably preceding new levels of volitional capacity and following as well. At any rate, among the products of the development of intentionality and volitional competency, if it is successful over a long period of time, is a *sense* of competency, pride of accomplishment, and the beginnings of self-respect. But, if this is one of the normal subjective products of autonomy, what is the comparable paranoid experience? *Where, for the normal person, autonomy brings a sense of competency, pride, and self-respect, the paranoid person, instead, is either arrogant and pseudo-competent or furtive and ashamed or, perhaps most often, both.*

The sense of shame seems, in fact, to be far more characteristic of paranoid people than, for example, the sense of guilt. Thus, they are ashamed, sometimes to the point of delusional preoccupation, about body odor, weak muscles, the shape of their nose, the size of their genitals, their lack of "manliness," the softness of their hands, and so forth. Although this feeling attaches typically to some external feature, one can be sure that it is actually quite pervasive and continuous and reflects a general lack of self-respect. Thus, one paranoid patient who felt particularly ashamed of his "baby hands" also felt ashamed of his "weakness" in general, his vulnerability to other people's evaluation of him, and even, in his words, his "lack of will."

There is, however, one other subjective reflection of the paranoid person's unstable autonomy. It is the most familiar of all. While the normal person feels not only competent, but also free to exercise his will, and, in that sense as well, self-directing, in charge of his own life, and, master of himself, the paranoid person is continuously occupied and concerned with the threat of being subjected to some external control or some external infringement of his will.

The development of intentionality and will has a double aspect or significance for every person's functioning. It has an internal significance such as I have described, and it has a decided significance for the individual's position vis-à-vis those around him. The emergence of intentionality and will in the child implies the simultaneous emergence of a new interest in self-determination, that is, freedom from external compulsion or force, in the child's relations with the external world. Any parent will easily confirm this fact. When the child learns that he can do something at will, he wants to do it according to *his* will. With the appearance of intentionality, volition, and will, or rather with each fresh increment of them, there is fresh interest in comparative power and strength and in the dimensions of domination and submission, compulsion and freedom. All these take on a significance that they did not have before. Indeed, a radical revision of relations with external figures of authority may easily be the most conspicuous objective manifestation of this internal change. For example, the child becomes stubborn or "negativistic," that is, unwilling to abandon his own intentions in the face of external pressure or punishment; he automatically opposes such pressure whenever he senses it. The appearance of obstinacy or negativism is based not only in instinctual developments, but also in fresh increments of the child's intentionality, volition, and competency. We describe this obstinacy in children as "willfulness" and quite properly so; the contests with various external figures that it invariably entails are, in actual fact and not only in common speech, contests of will, one basis of which, on the child's side, is a new sense of will and volitional competency.

Personal autonomy always retains this twofold aspect or reference. On the one hand, it has to do with the capacity for and interest in volitionally and competently directing one's self, one's own muscles, for example, as opposed to helplessness or passivity in this respect; on the other hand, it has to do with the capacity for and interest in directing oneself according to one's own will and independently of external force or authority. Since both these interests and capacities rely on the same psychological conditions, the form of one can always be expected to have its reflection in the other as well.

Thus, if autonomy, intentionality, or will is well established and stable, it can be relaxed in two senses. The normal person can not only relax his will sufficiently to allow spontaneity or abandonment, but also can relax his will, under reasonable circumstances, sufficiently to listen to, comply with, or even submit to the will of others. The normal person can, in other words, "give in" in both these senses. He can "give in" to himself without feeling anxiety, and he can "give in" to others without feeling humiliated or worse.

By the same token, where it is necessary to maintain rigid self-directedness, neither abandonment, that is, "giving in" to oneself, nor "giving in" to external pressure or authority can be tolerated. Furthermore, where rigid self-directedness is maintained only under great tension and is none too stable, one can expect not only resistance to external force or authority, but also acute awareness of it and sensitivity to it. Indeed, one could say that it is a peculiar feature of unstable autonomy that the threat of "giving in" to external domination and the threat of "giving in" to internal pressure (in the form of drives or affects) have a kind of subjective equivalence, since both involve a threat to the same psychological functions. At any rate, just such apprehensive, defensive, and ultimately antagonistic awareness of external authority and force does, in fact, pervade the paranoid person's subjective life. The manifestation vis-à-vis the external world of the paranoid person's continuous, rigidly maintained directedness of himself is a continuous and preoccupying concern with the defense of his autonomy against external assault.

The projective apprehensions of severely paranoid, psychotic, or borderline psychotic people, for example, are regularly and more or less explicitly concerned not merely with a general threat of external aggression, but with the more specific external threat of aggressive destruction or subjugation of will or intentional capacity.

Thus, a major category of paranoid delusions has to do with being directly controlled or immobilized by special or supernatural devices, machines, or powers possessed by enemies. For example, one such patient, who had suddenly become convinced that her companion was attempting to hypnotize her, started to phone for help only to be paralyzed hypnotically, according to her experience, and rendered unable to lift the receiver. Other patients, as is well known, experience their very thoughts as controlled by external devices.

Sometimes, in the projective idea, the concern involves not a direct assault on autonomy or subjugation of will by force or special power, but the insidious corruption or weakening of volition or will. This may be done by special chemicals, for example. One patient also believed that his will was being weakened and undermined by the "soft life" and those who practiced it at his university. Sometimes, a delusional idea of a weakened or deteriorating autonomy does not include any explicit reference to an external source or agent, as in the case of one paranoid schizophrenic patient who believed that he was gradually losing control of his sphincter muscles and "leaking" foul odors. Perhaps, in this case, an idea of an external source was developed later.

Essentially, the same themes, reflecting the same types of concerns, are to be found in the preoccupying ideas of less severe cases. The bitter resentment of being forced to submit to the authority or power of a boss, teacher, or officer; the fear of being induced or tricked into surrendering some element of self-determination, for example, by signing a contract; and the concern with being "forced" to surrender some freedom of action by rules or regulations will all be familiar characteristics to anyone who has known paranoid people. The same concerns are evident, also, in the continuous, everyday attitudes and frame of mind of paranoid characters. Thus, these people are, in general, extremely aware of power and rank, relative position, superior and inferior, who is boss and who is obliged to take orders, or who is in a position to humiliate whom. Many paranoid characters are more or less continuously involved, in subjective feeling and imagination if not actually, in some form of defensive and antagonistic engagement with one or another authority figure.

Sometimes, these people will be arrogant or cocky before such figures, and, sometimes, they will be furtive and ashamed. But, in either case, they will be defensively aware of being in the presence of authority. In the final analysis, a person of uncertain authority over himself and uncertain self-respect will, from his subjective viewpoint, regard figures of authority with a respect that is exorbitant. This essential fact is not changed by the circumstance that the uncertainty of autonomy is covered by a rigid self-directedness or that the lack of self-respect is masked by pseudocompetence or arrogance. These qualifications only guarantee that the respect these people have for rank and authority will not be friendly or appreciative respect, but defensive, grudging, and antagonistic; but it is respect nonetheless. It does not take deep or long observation to realize that even defensively arrogant paranoid characters who rail at the boss' stupidity and try to disparage him, no less than those who simply feel furtive and ashamed, respect the boss more than they respect themselves.

It is on account of this fact that even quite mildly paranoid people are not only wary before people of superior authority, but also are acutely concerned with the evaluation these people will make of them and are acutely sensitive to rebuff. Indeed, for these people, the simple awareness of attention from a person of rank seems to be the ingredient that is capable of precipitating a sharp sense of shame or humiliation out of a general absence of self-respect. The social discomfort and self-consciousness of many mildly paranoid people seem, similarly, to be based in such awareness—not only guarded awareness of exposure to ex-

ternal power, but also ashamed awareness of exposure to external rank.

In attempting to show that it is in the nature of a condition
of rigid, unstable autonomy to be defensively and antagonisti-
cally engaged, in various forms and degrees, with certain external figures and forces, I have drawn a picture that is, I am
aware, still quite incomplete. This picture omits projection,
without which the sense of paranoid mobilization cannot be
completely understood. But I have wanted to demonstrate, even
at the risk of taxing the reader with this incompleteness, that
certain essential aspects of paranoid functioning have psychological sources independent of projection, that they are not merely
results of projection, but may even be part of its foundation
even though, ultimately, this dependency may be completely
mutual.

Before concluding this section, I would like to say a few words
about another point that, to some readers, may also have been
rather conspicuously absent from our considerations so far. This
point concerns the significance, discovered by Freud and generally accepted since, of unconscious passive-homosexual drives in
paranoid functioning. Strictly speaking, this matter and the discussion here describe different dimensions of the problem of
paranoid functioning. The relationship between paranoia and
homosexuality is a dynamic one, paranoia being a defense
against homosexuality, whereas our interest is to understand the
general *forms* of paranoid functioning. Nevertheless, there is no
reason to avoid an interesting question where the two points of
view may have some bearing on one another. I have described
paranoid style, thus far, as involving a special kind of distortion
of normal autonomy, a distortion that implies certain weak-
nesses of autonomy. Can the source of this weakness of autonomy be identified as a compelling, unconscious, passive-homosexual impulse?

It is tempting to answer this question with a simple "yes,"

since that answer would immediately link much that has been said to a great deal of clinical observation and theoretical understanding. And such an answer would, in fact, not be difficult to support. One has only to imagine that what we call weakness or instability of autonomy, from a formal point of view, represents, from a motivational standpoint, a temptation to passive surrender. Indeed, there is no lack of evidence for just such underlying temptations in the defensive concerns and preoccupations I have described, such as concern with being immobilized, paralyzed, violated, and so forth. There is no doubt, either, that the temptation or impulse toward passive surrender will include, perhaps, even focus on—and, in men, possibly even invariably so—passive-homosexual impulses.

All this, I think, is on reasonably substantial ground, but the matter is more complicated than this. While the weakness of paranoid autonomy and the temptation to passive surrender that we may reasonably infer from it may generally include passive-homosexual impulses, it also includes more. The paranoid person dreads not only passive surrender as implied by passive-homosexual impulses, but also passive surrender of directedness and intentionality to *any* impulse. From this viewpoint, in other words, it is not only the drive content of homosexuality that the paranoid person dreads, but also the drive mode insofar as it is a mode of surrender. Insofar as abandonment to any impulse or even affect implies a surrender of directedness and intentionality, the paranoid person dreads it. Thus, one may easily observe paranoid people who are much more comfortable talking about their homosexuality than laughing about anything, for laughing always involves a certain degree of abandonment, whereas talking does not necessarily do so. It is not even difficult to imagine psychological circumstances where homosexual activity is not experienced subjectively as abandonment of directedness or intentionality or represents less of an abandonment than, for example, abandonment to intense aggressive impulses. It is well known, in fact, that some paranoid people do have quite conscious homosexual interests and even pursue overt homosexual activity. I cannot carry this interesting matter any further here, however, but refer the reader to the last chapter where their is some consideration of the general relationship between instinctual drives and style of functioning.

Projection: Noncognitive Aspects

Psychological functioning is a continuous process, but, in understanding some part of it, we often are obliged to disregard this continuity at some convenient point. Let me do this here with the following question. What are likely to be the results, what processes are likely to be set in motion, if the psychological organization that has been described so far is subjected to additional internal tension in the form, for example, of intensification of some repudiated or discomforting impulse or affect?

In a general way, the answer to this question is plain. Intensification of internal tension will place additional strain on the existing modes of tension control and result in intensification of them, as well as of other existing manifestations of tension or instability. Specifically, a rigid person, under the pressure of additional internal tension, will generally become more rigid. And a person who is not only rigid, but also defensive, will, under additional tension, become more defensive as well.

Let me describe this process in another, more psychological way. It is a special fact of the psychology of a person of rigid, unstable autonomy that he must always defend that autonomy on two fronts at the same time. He must defend it against internal and external threat. The battle on the one front results in rigidity; that on the other front in defensiveness. Because of this special fact of engagement on two fronts at the same time, any weakening of or threat to autonomy that originates internally will necessarily intensify the sense of vulnerability to external threat as well, and it is likely, therefore, to result in intensification not only of rigidity, but also of defensiveness. These rather

unremarkable facts are, it seems to me, central to the understanding of paranoid functioning in general and projection in
particular, for they describe a process by which, in an individual
characterized by a certain mode of functioning, intensification
of internal tension has the result, in part, of intensification of
defensive tension vis-à-vis the external world. They describe the
first step of a process by which an internal tension may be transformed by a certain psychological organization into an external
one.

For example, a rather rigid and defensive man happens to ad-
mire his boss, although he is usually stiff and uneasy in the boss'
presence. He would like to invite the boss to dinner at his home,
an idea that feels quite daring to him, however. He no sooner
plans this invitation than he experiences an intensification of his
usual defensive concern with what the boss thinks of him and with
the possibility of rebuff. In the days preceding the invitation, he
is stiffer, more sensitive, and more defensively alert in the boss'
presence than ever before. An internal tension has given rise to an
intensified defensive sensitivity and tension vis-à-vis an external
figure.

For a paranoid person, however, the process that begins with
the transformation of internal tension into intensified defensive
concern and intensified sense of vulnerability does not end at
this point. For a paranoid person, intensification of defensive
tension means automatic intensification of the whole paranoid
apparatus of mobilization, including, particularly, the cognitive
apparatus. Under the impetus of an intensified sense of vulnerability and fresh defensive tension, the whole rigid, mobilized
mode of functioning, which had been momentarily disconcerted
by an internal tension, is now revived, equipped with a fresh
defensive aim, and directed toward a fresh external object. At
this point, such a person can no longer be described as feeling
vulnerable or as defensively sensitive; now, he is sharp-eyed and
alert, actively identifying the enemy, anticipating and interpreting his moves, and constructing an image from clues noted ac-

cording to his defensive interest. In a word, he is now suspicious, and the outcome of his suspiciousness will be a projection.

The following is a quite condensed account of the development of some projective ideas from feelings that were in some respects similar to those in the example above but in a somewhat more rigid and paranoid character.

A very intelligent thirty-three-year-old college professor, stiff and self-conscious but also quite ambitious and sometimes rather arrogant, had always been sensitive to any rebuff or slight to his dignity, to being "forced" or ordered to do anything arbitrarily, or otherwise treated, as it seemed to him, like a "kid." In this instance, he had recently taken a new job with a different institution and had become interested, although ashamed to admit it, in impressing an important senior professor, obviously with the hope of becoming a protegé of his and probably also with the idea of ultimately outstripping him. At any rate, he was initially quite impressed with this man, and, consequently, he was quite nervous in his presence and concerned with what the older man might think of him. Sometimes, he was concerned that he might be thought "weak" while, at other times, too self-aggrandizing. He watched for signs of both reactions.

So far, this intensification of defensive tension, including the intensified sense of vulnerability and defensive concern, may still be regarded as preprojective. However, it soon became clear that this defensive tension and intensified sense of vulnerability was gradually giving rise to an intensification of rigidity and an increasingly antagonistic defensive stiffening. Thus, he not only watched for signs of rebuff or disapproval, but also increasingly anticipated them and, accordingly, braced himself with each hesitant overture. He remembered now that he despised fawning yes-men, and, therefore, he now approached the older man only in a determinedly dignified and equalitarian way.

In the course of some weeks, apparently marked mostly by indifference on the side of the older man, this defensive stiffening progressed further. He watched the older man closely now, no longer with concern, but with suspicion. He angrily seized on some quite ambiguous evidence of disparaging slights and arbitrary, commanding attitudes on the senior man's part. He would not "take it," and he frequently became not merely equalitarian, but defensively arrogant in the relationship. Thus, he refused "menial" department assignments. Once angry and suspicious, he began to watch the colleague, in the way such people do, like a small boy playing cops and robbers around an unconcerned father, only with much more intensity and seriousness, interpreting each movement according to the game—now he is pretending not to notice me, now he is getting ready to shoot, and so on. From this angry, suspicious, and, by now, defensively quite haughty view, he discovered clues that showed him that he had been right; the older man resented his independence, wanted only a mediocre yes-man in the department, and was trying to reduce him to that status. He declared that the situation between them had now come to a "contest of wills."

The activation of paranoid defensive mobilization under the impetus of fresh discomfort or an intensified sense of vulnerability implies more than the activation of suspicious attention. It means total stiffening into that intense, single-minded directedness of which these people are capable and, under that regime that now has a fresh defensive aim, further contraction of affective experience, tightening of the sense of self into a command headquarters, and, therefore, further estrangement of the paranoid person from his own underlying affects and impulses. These two aspects of the defensive stiffening—intensification of suspicious attention directed toward the identification of an external enemy, on the one hand, and simultaneous loss of internal experience, on the other—obviously work in the same direction.

In all likelihood, some background awareness of one's own feelings and interests provides an anchorage for the normal process of empathic imagination. A continuous sense of one's own feelings must, in other words, be one factor that keeps the normal person from losing himself in his empathic imaginings of another's feelings. Without such an anchorage, the paranoid person is able not only to construct an image of the enemy from clues seized according to the direction of his defensive bias, but also to regard that image with an attitude of cold objectivity and with no recognition at all of himself in it. In this respect, he is perhaps in the position of the passenger on a train who, if his attention is fixed on another train alongside and if in addition he does not experience a sensation of his own motion, cannot realize that it is *his* train that is moving.

The general understanding of projection that I am proposing here can be summarized by the following diagram:

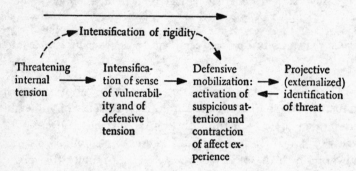

It is best to conceive of the process as having two stages. In the first, a repudiated impulse or a discomforting affect or idea threatens an already rigid and defensive organization, intensifies feelings of vulnerability and defensive sensitivity, and automatically exacerbates both rigidity and defensive mobilization. In the second and more properly projective stage, the paranoid individual, now more rigidly and defensively mobilized, suspicious and seizing clues according to his defensive aims, identifies the enemy and constructs the concrete external threat. I have tried to indicate by the double arrows in the last step of the diagram the interdependence and continued interplay between the paranoid person's state of defensive mobilization, on the one hand, and the object of this mobilization, that is, his projective image of the actual external object, on the other. While the projective object is largely a creation of his defensive tension and the stiffening of defensive processes, once created and even as it crystallizes, it will itself continue to focus that tension and consolidate the defensive mobilization further. Sometimes, one can observe this process along with the crystallization of a projective idea not all in one stroke, but, as in the mild example cited above, first in a general and sketchy outline and then, as the paranoid person gets the scent, filled in with detail and logical connection.

This whole process, once under way, is intrinsically progressive and self-completing, and it is so for a quite simple reason. It is subjectively relieving. It accomplishes, after all, not only a transformation of an internal into an external tension, but also, more specifically, a transformation of a tension that is disorganizing and noxious to a tight, rigidly directed psychological system into one that constitutes a fresh object for that directedness.

I believe that this general conception will show certain of the clinical features of projection in a clearer light. I have in mind, for example, the fact that projective ideas always seem to involve an aspect of self-reference. Let me explain my point. Even though projection is sometimes described as a process of "expulsion" of mental contents, we know that, in actual practice, this description is not adequate. The fact is that mental contents are not simply "expelled" or attributed to an external object, with that being the end of it. The process always involves not only a direction from subject to external object, but also, in subjective experience, a direction back from object to subject, most typically, in the form of an experience of some threat or antagonistic force directed by the external object toward the subject. We have no reason to consider this aspect of the process as secondary or incidental. Observation shows us, in other words, that, in projection, internal tensions are not "expelled," but are transformed into continuing tensions vis-à-vis the external world. Thus, a continuing dynamic relationship between the subject and the object—for example, between persecuted and persecutor—is never absent from the total projective experience and is generally manifest in the content of the projective idea.

Why should this be so? According to our viewpoint, the essential nature of projection, what it is all about, makes it so. The fact that projective ideas have an aspect of self-reference simply reflects their psychological history and function. It reflects that such ideas are based, in the first place, on a transformation of internal tension into defensive tension, that the process of projection owes its existence to an original defensive sensitivity and relationship to the external world, and that it continues and extends that relationship autistically, absorbing internal tension in the process. From this standpoint, therefore, we must say that "self-reference" is merely the term used to describe one aspect, one of the two directions, so to speak, of what remains an essentially defensive relationship between the subject and an external object; for example, we will regard even the self-reference of the delusion of persecution as having its psychological roots in the defensive sensitivity of a condition of rigid, unstable autonomy.

We come now to a more general problem concerning projection and projective content and, I believe, also to some further conclusions. The problem is this. There are, actually, two common definitions of paranoid projection that, as far as I can tell, are used interchangeably in psychiatry and psychoanalysis. According to the first, projection is the attribution of objectionable motives, affects, or ideas of one's own to an external object. This definition is the basis of the "expulsion" view of projection. According to the second, projection is the substitution of an (apparently) external threat or tension for an internal one. Thus, the first definition says that the content or the idea of the internal tension or threat is projected, whereas the second says that the threat or tension is projected, and a substitute experience is achieved. Of course, these two definitions are used interchangeably because it is assumed that they are equivalent and come to the same thing. It is assumed that the experience of externalized threat follows simply from the attribution to the external object of the content of the tension that is internally threatening. In actual fact, however, this assumption is not warranted, and the two definitions are not equivalent.

In the first place, it simply does not follow that the attribution to an external figure of mental contents identical to those that are internally threatening *would* invariably result in a substitute experience of external threat. Why should it? One might easily imagine that the external figure to whom objectionable characteristics or motives have been attributed—for example, *he* is a homosexual, he is aggressive, or the like—would be regarded as objectionable and, on that account, would be repudiated. But that is not what we observe. All that we observe of paranoid projection tells us, on the contrary, that the external projective object becomes not merely objectionable, but also an apparent source of aggressive threat directed actively at the subject.

Conversely, if an external object is to be endowed with attributes such that it does come to represent a threat or tension that corresponds to or substitutes for the original internal threat or tension, we have no reason to assume, *a priori*, that the content of those attributes would invariably need to be identical with the contents of the original internal tension or threat. When we reckon the value of an object in a foreign currency, we do not assume that it can be expressed in the same number of pesos or marks that it costs in dollars. We understand that a different system, a different money language, is involved, and, in order to represent the value correctly, we must translate it into that new system. If we insist otherwise, we confuse money language with value.

According to our view and, I believe, according to the evidence, it is the tension and the threat that are invariably and essentially transferred and externalized in projection; they achieve a substitute form in the experience of the projective object but not necessarily by the reproduction of their contents in the attributes of that object. If, however, the projective contents, that is, the attributes projectively assigned to the external object, are not necessarily those of the original internal tension, what do they consist of and how are they determined? In our view, the internal tension achieves externalized form, first, by transformation into defensive tension and, then, by projective reconstruction. The projective content will, therefore, be generally determined by the content of the defensive tension. More exactly, those contents will be attributed to the external object by a process of interpretation of selected clues that satisfy and crystallize the particular defensive anticipations of the given state of defensive tension. It is true, as this works out, that, in certain types of instance, the ultimate projective content will be virtually identical with that of the internal tension that gave rise to it; but this is not invariably the case, and, in general, it cannot be assumed to be the case.

Let me illustrate the point with an instance of both types. First, a commonplace and mild type of projection, where the projective content is virtually identical with that of the tension that gave rise to it.

An actually quite competent and well-respected man, who was, however, not convinced of his own competency and was defensive about his professional rank and status in his firm, made a mistake in his work. It was a mistake of no great consequence, easily corrected, and hardly likely to be noticed by anyone else. Nevertheless, for some days afterwards, he was preoccupied with imagining even the most remote possibilities of being discovered and the humiliation that would, according to him, follow from discovery. During this time, when the boss walked by, he "noticed" an irritable glance and imagined the boss to be thinking, "This man is the weak link in our organization."

In general, externalizations of self-critical ideas or self-critical evaluations, including all those projections that are usually described as "superego projections," are likely to reproduce the content and even the language of the original internal tension quite literally and directly. There is a special reason for this, which has to do with the nature of that original tension and its position, so to speak, in the psychological organization. In these cases, the fact that the internal tension is a self-critical idea means that it has a quasi-external form, subjectively speaking, in the first place and, indeed, that the subjective attitude toward that self-critical idea or thought—for example, the "voice" of one's conscience—is already quasi-defensive before projection. Consequently, the defensive transformation of such an internal tension, the intensification of defensive tension, and then the projective construction of a substitute external threat is, in this case, an exceptionally abbreviated and simple one. It requires only the attribution to an external figure of the words of an already quasi-external "inner voice."

In the second example, which follows, the same process of externalization of tension and threat is accomplished only by a radical alteration in content.

A somewhat masculine and tomboyish girl in her twenties, a patient in an open psychiatric sanatorium, was continually concerned with the danger and the disgrace of "giving in" to authority or compulsion. She guarded both her independence of decision and her freedom of movement (including, literally, the keys to her car) very closely. On the whole, therefore, she maintained a careful distance from most of the institution's programs and personnel and, in some cases, not only distance, but also an attitude of cold war.

On various occasions, however, she was clearly tempted to relax her usual guardedness, to admit that she enjoyed some institutional activity, to lose interest in her ever ready plans to depart the place, or to do something that she thought might please her therapist. Such occasions were likely to be followed by sharp intensification of her usual defensive concerns, eventuating in the projective "discovery" of motives or plans to "trap" her in the sanatorium, to brainwash her, or in some way to induce her to "surrender." These ideas, in turn, were often followed by wild, rebellious actions.

In such a case, therefore, a variety of repudiated passive temptations may intensify defensive concerns with giving in and the sense of vulnerability to external compulsion and lead, thus, to the projective construction of an aggressive external threat.[3] The projec-

---

[3] It is interesting to note that, in the case of a female, the paranoid condition is also associated with undoubtedly homosexual tendencies. But

tive external threat of destruction of autonomy that corresponds to and substitutes for the original internal threat of the temptation to relax her guarded self-directedness necessarily has a different manifest content.

In asserting that projection achieves an external substitute for or psychological equivalent of internal tension or threat and does not necessarily reproduce the idea or content of that threat in the attributes of the external object, I believe that I am satisfying the sense, if not completely the letter, of the psychoanalytic conception of projection. It should be noted that, in actual practice, it is perfectly well known that projective content does not necessarily duplicate the content of the original internal tension. We do not imagine, for instance, that the projective idea of being trapped reflects, literally, a repudiated motive to trap. Specific psychoanalytic formulations of the projection of various internal tensions have always taken certain transformations of content into account or taken them for granted. Nevertheless, it seems to me that, because of theoretical confusions, account has not been taken of the fact that certain transformations of content are intrinsic to the projective process itself, that is, intrinsic to the externalization of *tension* and, therefore, do not need to be attributed to additional or supplemental mental operations.

The last case cited illustrates another point concerning the nature of projective content. I have in mind the relationship, especially evident in this case, between the particular nature of the individual's defensive orientation, on the one hand, and the content of his projective ideas, on the other.

Thus, this patient had always been especially sensitive to any infringement on her freedom of physical movement. The impor-

---

it appears that it is not the homosexual, that is, masculine, inclination that is repudiated, but, as in the case of a man, the passive feminine temptations to surrender that are repudiated, as it were, from a masculine point of view.

tance of this particular dimension of autonomy is evidenced not only by what she said, but also by the special value and necessity to her of a car, her obvious satisfaction in using it, and, perhaps, her general athletic and boyish physical style. When this patient projectively constructs an external threat under conditions of special tension, it is the threat of being "trapped."

Let me try to make my point clear. If the projective process depends on the intensification of defensive tension and the activation of defensive psychological processes, then it follows that the ultimate specific projective content is dependent on two variables: first, the specific nature of the original internal tension and, second, the specific nature of the individual's defensive concerns, attitudes, and orientation. Projection substitutes an external threat for an internal one, but paranoid individuals are not all of one mind as to precisely what constitutes an external threat. The subjective definition of external threat, the determination of what constitutes such a threat and in what particular way, depends on the nature of the defensive disposition the individual maintains vis-à-vis the external world. In turn, it will determine, for any given internal tension, the particular nature of suspicious anticipations and, therefore, of the projective content. Thus, in the presence of some figure of impressive authority, one mildly paranoid person, always concerned with his standing in the eyes of such people, anticipates a humiliating rebuff; another, more furtive and antagonistic, stiffens and anticipates being caught at something; and still another, perhaps more rigidly defensive of his dignity, ambitious, and lofty, becomes loftier still and ready for contest as he projectively sees in the other's eyes the motive to put him in his place. Each one experiences intensification of vulnerability and defensive tension, stiffens defensively vis-à-vis the external figure, and projectively identifies a concrete external threat according to how he feels vulnerable and what, from the standpoint of his particular defensive orientation, would constitute such a threat.

Let me give another set of examples.

One paranoid patient, a rather frail looking young man, had always been extremely shy and had suffered from the most acute sense of shame and self-consciousness for many years. From this defensive standpoint of looking up to his betters for their critical evaluation of him, he developed, in a state of decompensation, the delusional idea that other patients in the sanatorium regarded him with disgust, thought that he was a homosexual and that he smelled bad, and were "shunning" him for these reasons.

On the other hand, an arrogantly righteous and self-willed young man, also in a state of decompensation and also concerned about homosexuality, characteristically attempted an attitude of disdainful aloofness toward other patients in the sanatorium. He also felt vulnerable, but, from his lofty standpoint—still contemptuous, although now also angry, and, altogether like the lion irritated with hyenas—he remarked coldly that certain of those "spoiled brats" were obviously trying to "provoke" him and "had better watch their step."

It is not possible to give more than a sample here of what are innumerable differences in defensive orientation among paranoid people. They include differences both in level of defensive concern—such as between concern with external critical evaluation and concern with external force or compulsion—and differences in type of defensive orientation—such as between a furtive orientation and an arrogant one. One could, no doubt, classify the differences along other dimensions as well. My point, however, is only to suggest a general principle, namely, that all variations in defensive orientation result in corresponding variations in projective content.

Thus far, we have regarded projection essentially as a particular and sporadic process, one that restores comparative stability to a rigid and defensive system when it is threatened and made more vulnerable by special temptation, impulse, or self-critical doubt. But we might easily reason that the various instances of special tension that seem to provide the impetus for particular projections are, after all, only especially intense instances of what must essentially be continuous and continuously threatening internal tensions. As a matter of fact, we have good reason to believe—for example, from the general content of their imaginative productions—that these rigid, defensive people function under the continuous pressure of especially unmodulated impulses and affects. Along with the continuous threat of internal tension and, more immediately, along with the intensified sense of vulnerability and defensive tension that it is likely to continually produce in this context, one can imagine only a more or less continuous projective motive or interest. In actual fact, we know that, in paranoid conditions and especially in the so-called paranoid characters, projection is by no means only an occasional process, but is a constant and in some instances actually continuous one.

It is true that, in some respects, the process of projection seems to be intrinsically discontinuous. Defensive tension builds, suspiciousness grows, an external and more manageable threat is constructed, and, in a sense, the process has reached its natural end. As a rule, what we see of projections does have this form. We see specific projective ideas emerge under conditions of tension, and, unless the condition deteriorates, we frequently see them fade, sometimes simply when the individual removes himself from the circumstances and the particular projective object that is involved.

But we know, in the first place, that this is not always the case and, second, that it is rarely the end of it. Thus, sometimes specific projective ideas will become a more or less permanent part of the individual's psychology. Some of the so-called "encapsulated" delusions are conspicuous, if extreme, examples of this. There are also other, less striking ways in which projective ideas and preoccupations can become more or less permanently established, such as by being incorporated into social attitudes or convictions or into images of whole groups or classes of people or of social institutions. Many paranoid characters, no doubt, are to be found among the adherents of fanatical and witch-hunting political or quasipolitical movements, preoccupied with the defense of our country against those who would "poison its water supply" by fluoridation, pollute its racial purity, undermine its "will to resist," or the like. Aside, however, from such relatively permanently established ideas, we know that, when projection does fade from interest with a change of scene, for example, it is very likely to have faded only temporarily, and shortly, in the new job or the new city, closely similar ideas will begin to develop. Among some paranoid characters, there seem to be unending successions of projective engagements, one fading only to be immediately replaced by a new one, much in the way obsessional people abandon one worry only to turn promptly to another. Sometimes, these people seem to live a constant round of battles with a series of bosses or fussy, suspicious disputes with neighbors, with other patients in a hospital, or with hospital authorities.

Still, such constant, full-blown projective engagements are by no means characteristic of all paranoid characters, nor even, probably, of most. Among most paranoid characters, there are only sporadic flareups of projective ideas and defensive mobilization; yet, in the periods in between such flareups, there is no real demobilization, but only a subsiding to a somewhat lower level of defensive tension and projective experience. These are the people who are characterized, for the most part, by a continuous, alert guardedness. This state, which probably is the most general condition of paranoid characters, is, in other words, a state of truly continuous projective experience. But it is a kind of projective experience that has certain special features and deserves a few words more.

When we say that a person is guarded in his attitude, we mean that he takes precautions, that he maintains himself continuously in a state of readiness for threat or awareness of its possibility. Thus, the guarded person is not necessarily convinced of the current existence of threat, but he does believe in the necessity of maintaining a continuous awareness of the possibility of it, even when he sees no sign of it. This is not strange when we take account of the special bias that his subjective circumstances impose on him. From the standpoint of a vulnerable man, the possibility of threat and the possibility of its absence do not have equal weight. The one possibility is definite reason for concern, but the mere possibility of the absence of threat is no reason for relaxation. To such a person, ambiguity or even apparent innocence is no reassurance. On the contrary, only the identification of a threat can be decisive, while the apparent absence of threat only requires continuous readiness for it.

Thus, the guarded person exists in a continuous state of projective awareness but not necessarily projective experience of full intensity. The aim of guardedness is not different, except perhaps in degree, from the aim of suspiciousness or projective attention in general. Its aim is *not* to avoid threat, but to avoid *vulnerability* to threat—being surprised by it or passive before it. Whereas, in regular projection, under the pressure of greater defensive tension, this aim can only be accomplished by positively identifying a threat, in guardedness, it is sufficiently accomplished by continuous awareness of its possibility. From this standpoint, the condition of guardedness, for many and perhaps most paranoid characters, seems to represent, as it were, a continuous baseline of defensive tension and projective experience. Intensity of defensive mobilization and definiteness of projective construction of external threat can rise instantly and sharply above this baseline, and they do with any intensification of internal tension or aggravating external circumstance or, for that matter, with even a hint of actual threat. But they cannot fall below this line except momentarily and then with immediate discomfort and experience of vulnerability. In mild cases, particularly, the possibility of threat need not be continuously in the focus of awareness. It is necessary only that it never be completely out of awareness, that it never be completely forgotten, that the guarded person never completely relax.

If the possibility of threat does disappear from the attention of a guarded person—and this does happen momentarily even with the most guarded and paranoid people—it is striking to see that discomforting ideas, like small signals of vulnerability, immediately emerge. Thus, these people remember in the nick of time that their smile looks ridiculous, or that to buy a tie like the boss' will really look like childish aping, or that to agree too quickly is really what yes-men do. With these ideas, the condition of guardedness is reinstated, and further experience of vulnerability, and more, is forestalled.

The Relationship between Paranoid and Obsessive-Compulsive Styles

In the introductory chapter, I suggested that an examination of general forms of functioning or styles might throw some light on the relationships between certain pathological conditions that, while quite disparate in ordinary psychiatric description, seem to be very closely associated empirically. Paranoid and obsessive-compulsive conditions are an outstanding example of such association. It is well known, for instance, how often the premorbid background of a paranoid decompensation will turn out to be an obsessive-compulsive and, particularly, an obsessional character. Even more convincing evidence of a close affinity between the two conditions is offered by the existence of certain borderline psychotic states, sometimes described as over-ideational pre(paranoid) schizophrenic states, in which obsessional and paranoid features seem to intermingle and to shade into one another. In such conditions, it is difficult, for example, to say whether the elaborate intellectualizing that is one of the most conspicuous features of this state should be regarded as obsessional or paranoid.

The diagnostic labels themselves are of little importance; what is interesting is the similarity of form that such a puzzle and such a gradual transition indicates. No such affinity is especially indicated by the names we give to the defense mechanisms, traits, or symptoms respectively characteristic of each, but even the briefest examination of formal qualities confirms it, in my opinion, unmistakably. Such an examination shows not merely that the two styles are alike, for their differences are obviously at least as critical as their resemblances, but also that there is a close and definite relationship between them, virtually every formal aspect of the one style bearing a relationship to a corresponding aspect of the other.

For the sake of conciseness and also for ease of comparison I have presented various features of their correspondence in Tables 1 and 2. Table 1 deals with the two styles of cognition; Table 2 deals with more general aspects of the two styles, re-

Table 1

Comparison of Obsessive-Compulsive and Paranoid Styles: Cognition

	Mode of attention	Object of attention	Response to the novel or unexpected	Experience of reality
Obsessive-compulsive	Acute, intense, and narrowly focused; fixed on what is relevant to its own idea and interest Characterization: rigid	Technical detail	Refuses attention; the unexpected regarded as distraction from own fixed line of thought	World constructed of technical indicators; loss of sense of conviction and sense of substantial truth; extreme manifestation is logical absurdity
Paranoid	Extremely acute, intense, and narrowly focused; fixed on its own idea, searching only confirmation; biased Characterization: suspicious	The clue	Sharply attentive but not to apparent content ("mere appearance"); searches out confirming clue to "real" meaning; the unexpected regarded as threatening	World constructed of clues to hidden meaning; apparent, substantial reality disdained; extreme manifestation is projective delusion

Table 2

Comparison of Obsessive-Compulsive and Paranoid Styles: Behavior and Subjective Experience

	General behavior mode	Response to external influence	Affective experience	Sense of pressure
Obsessive-compulsive	Rigid, tense, continuously and intensely directed, purposeful; general aim is accomplishment of work	Imperturbable, determinedly self-willed; obstinate, if pressed	Narrowing of subjective experience in general; narrowing of and estrangement from affective experience particularly (isolation of affect); loss of spontaneity, absence of whim; tense	Lives continuously under pressure of conscience, feeling of "should," experienced as quasi-external but superior to his wants; general reaction is ambivalent submission to authoritative (moral) principle
Paranoid	Continuous, tense, and antagonistic directedness, intentionality, purposefulness; "operating;" general aim is defense against threat	Touchy, guarded, suspicious	General contraction of subjective experience, probably some loss of sensual experience, narrowing of and complete estrangement from much affect (as in projection); loss of capacity for spontaneity and abandonment; extremely tense and usually antagonistic	Lives with awareness of threat of superior force or authority; threat experienced as external; general reaction is defensive

spectively. I assume it will be clear that I do not offer the tables as in any way exhaustive or necessarily presenting the most basic and essential aspects of this formal correspondence. They present only those particular affinities of form that have emerged and have seemed striking to me in the course of the individual studies of each style. So I present them neither to prove nor to define the relationship between the two styles, but only to suggest its existence and its nature.

Here are two styles, each of which is characterized by rigid and tense hypertrophy of normal functions and subjective experiences of autonomy. Each style, in its typical manifestation, includes a special and touchy mindfulness of the right of self-determination; each is peculiarly uninfluenceable and marked by special willfulness and tense, unrelenting purposiveness and self-direction; and, yet, each involves the special experience of living in the company of some external or quasi-external, superior, and/or threatening voice. Between these two styles, the paranoid is, in every instance, the more extreme, the less stable, the more tense and antagonistic, the more openly occupied with instinctual conflict, and, in a word, the more psychologically primitive.

I am suggesting, in other words, that, from the standpoint of form, the paranoid style may be regarded as a more primitive transformation, in the mathematical sense, of the obsessive-compulsive style. While I am only too well aware of the limitations of such a characterization of that transformation, I am hopeful that it adds some degree of reasonableness to the apparent facts—as, for instance, the fact that, under whatever the conditions are that produce such changes, when an obsessive-compulsive person does decompensate severely, it is quite likely to be in a paranoid direction.

4

Hysterical Style

In the current understanding of the operation of various neuroses, revolving in large part around the nature of the defense mechanisms considered to be more or less specific to each of them, the picture of hysterical neurosis is relatively clear-cut. It was the first neurotic condition to be studied by Freud, and, among neuroses, none has been more definitely or clearly associated with the operation of a specific defense mechanism than has hysteria with repression. The relative simplicity of this association becomes evident if, for example, it is compared with the constellation of defense mechanisms usually considered to be operative in obsessive-compulsive pathology—namely, regression, reaction-formation, isolation of affect, and undoing.

The mechanism of repression, furthermore, has a simplicity and clarity that is unique among the various defense mechanisms. It was, along with hysterical pathology, the first defense to be studied, and it retains a basic or elemental quality among the mechanisms, which cover a considerable range in both complexity and clarity. The mechanism of repression and its significance in hysterical pathology are, therefore, clear enough and, undoubtedly, real enough.

Yet, even in this case, there are legitimate reasons for doubt whether the specific defense mechanism of repression can by itself explain the shape or form of hysterical symptoms and traits, not to mention the typical constellations of attitudes and adaptive capacities that are associated with these symptoms and traits. And even if it could, how can we explain the reliance on this particular mechanism in this particular kind of person? We will, then, look for the matrix, the general ways of functioning, from which the specific operation of repression *as well as* other hysterical characteristics may arise.

Repression and the Hysterical Style of Cognition

There is a special reason for taking the mode of cognition as a starting point for a discussion of hysteria; it has to do with the nature of the concept of repression. Repression was defined by Anna Freud as "the withholding or expulsion of an idea or affect from the conscious ego." [1] But the repression we are most familiar with and what we most often mean by repression is forgetting—the loss not of affect, but of *ideational* contents from consciousness, the failure of once-perceived contents to achieve the status of conscious memories or of memories available to consciousness. It would seem that, among the various defense mechanisms, repression must be especially closely related to the process and mode of cognition. It is likely, in other words, that the qualities of memory and the conditions of forgetting are closely related to the mode of prior learning and attention.

I have not discussed thus far (and will have no occasion to discuss later) the special qualities of memory function that may be associated respectively with the various styles of functioning, but some of these, at least, are quite well known. Obsessive-compulsive people, for instance, are generally recognized as having "good," that is, technical and factual, memories. In certain

---

[1] Anna Freud, *The Ego and the Mechanisms of Defense* (London: Hogarth Press and Institute of Psychoanalysis, 1937), p. 55.

respects, in fact, their memory seems to be, if anything, superior to "normal" memory. It is commonplace, for instance, for obsessive-compulsive patients in psychotherapy to recall their childhood in great detail. That the obsessive-compulsive's memory is usually factual or "objective," with an abundance of technical detail, only suggests what one might guess in any case: that the content of recollection can hardly be independent of the nature of the original cognition and, further, that the style of recollection is likely to be consistent with the style of cognition in general—in this case, sharply focused, technical-factual apprehension of the world.

I am suggesting a twofold relationship between recollection and original cognition. The first aspect of this relationship consists simply in the fact that original cognition, including the organization of the cognitive data at the time, provides the material on which the recollection must draw. Recollection certainly need not and hardly can be identical in its content with the original cognition, but, on the other hand, it certainly must be limited by it.[2] In the case of the obsessive-compulsive, therefore, the sharply defined, technical data and organization of the original cognition provides the material on which recollection draws. But, in addition, it would be difficult to imagine that the process of recollection—the organizing and assembling of memories and the concentration of attention on them—is unrelated to the style of the original cognitive process. It seems much more plausible that essentially the same style of functioning of attention, for example, would operate in both the original cognition and the recollection.[3]

If it is true that the detailed, technical cognition of the obses-

---

[2] A good example of this limitation would be a person's incapacity to recollect details of a period of intoxication. I will leave aside, in this discussion, the matter of subliminal cognition.

[3] See, in this connection, the experimental work of I. H. Paul, "Studies in Remembering: The Reproduction of Connected and Extended Verbal Material," *Psychological Issues* I, Whole No. 2 (1959).

sive-compulsive and his sharply focused mode of attention are conducive to a "good" memory and, as I also suppose, *are not conducive to the repression of memory contents*, is it possible that the mode of cognition of hysterical people is, by its nature, particularly conducive to forgetting and the operation of repression? I will try to show that this is so, that the nature of hysterical thinking provides the groundwork for forgetting and makes it, in fact, inevitable. Let us now consider some of these qualities of hysterical cognition and thinking.

When a hysterical person is asked to describe someone else, the response is likely to be something like, "Oh, he's so big!" or "She's wonderful!" or "I hate him!" The quality of these perceptions can be conveyed more sharply if one makes an imaginary comparison with the factual, technically detailed answers that an obsessive person is likely to give to the same kind of question. When one asks a question of a hysterical person, in other words, one is likely to get for an answer not facts, but impressions. These impressions may be interesting and communicative, and they are very often vivid, but they remain impressions—not detailed, not quite sharply defined, and certainly not technical.

Once, for example, in taking a case history from an exceedingly hysterical patient, I made repeated efforts to obtain a description of her father from her.[4] She seemed, however, hardly to understand the sort of data I was interested in, and the best she could provide was, "My father? He was wham-bang! That's all—just wham-bang!"

I am suggesting that hysterical cognition in general is global, relatively diffuse, and lacking in sharpness, particularly in sharp detail. In a word, it is *impressionistic*. In contrast to the active, intense, and sharply focused attention of the obsessive-

---

[4] Let me mention at this point that the illustrations in this chapter reflect the fact that hysterics are preponderantly women. See the discussion on pages 180–181.

compulsive, hysterical cognition seems relatively lacking in sharp focus of attention; in contrast to the compulsive's active and prolonged searching for detail, the hysterical person tends cognitively to respond quickly and is highly susceptible to what is immediately impressive, striking, or merely obvious.

These same characteristics are evident in the Rorschach test.

Where the compulsive person carefully delineates a feature of anatomy, the hysteric looks quickly and exclaims, "It's bloody!" Where (as in the complex and brightly colored card X) the compulsive person may list and actively organize relations between varieties of botanical or marine specimens, the hysterical person says, "A beautiful bouquet," or "It's Paris! . . . like in the French Line posters." Where, even in the case of a rather obvious image (such as the "bat" on card I), the compulsive person may say, ". . . the outspread winglike areas and what might be taken for legs there and the head . . . of course, these look like antennae, which wouldn't be right, but still on the whole it most resembles a bat," the hysterical person glances at the card and says, "Oh! A big bat! Take it away!"

There is, in Rorschach testing, a technical procedure that is of special interest in connection with the relationship between recollection and original cognition. This is the procedure called "inquiry" in which, after the original responses have been given, the examiner questions the subject about various aspects of his responses without the cards being visible to him. The characteristic differences between hysterical people and obsessive-compulsives in their response to these questions are as conspicuous as the differences between their original perceptions. The obsessive-compulsive, in general, gives factual, technical answers of the sort I have already indicated. Hysterical people, although they do not usually forget their responses, are quite often unable to answer with any clarity such questions as, "What made it look like a bat?" Sometimes, they consider for a moment and give such a reply as, "Well, I don't know . . . it just did." Sometimes, even the sense or meaning of the question seems beyond them, not because of a lack of intelligence, but rather because it calls for the sort of technical facts or data that they are not prepared to give or that they do not clearly understand. They say, "What do you mean? It just *was* a bat. That's all." One could say, perhaps, that this type of response reflects only the incapacity of these people for technical introspection, which certainly is a fact; but the immediate and impressionistic qualities of their original perceptions suggest that, in addition to the problem of introspection, the original cognition did not include the sort of sharply defined, technical data that would make these questions easier to answer.

This lack of factual detail and sharp definition in hysterical cognition can hardly be attributed to the operation of the defense mechanism of repression. It is not a matter of the exclusion of specific ideational or emotional contents from consciousness and does not principally have to do with the contents of thought at all. It is a *form* of cognition, although, to be sure, it is a form that is often likely to result in vagueness or diffuseness—even barrenness—of clear, sharp thought *content*.

I would like to indicate some other manifestations and consequences of this style of cognition, each of which will receive further discussion later on. As typical hysterical traits, they will probably be familiar. It is my interest, however, to point out that they are aspects of a general mode of cognition. The first of these is the hysterical incapacity for persistent or intense intellectual concentration; the second is the distractibility or impressionability that follows from it; and the third is the nonfactual world in which the hysterical person lives.

First, consider the incapacity for concentration. It is striking to see, when a hysterical person is asked to solve a mathematics problem on a psychological test, that she looks at it as though hoping to be inspired with an answer, and ultimately she guesses. It is an advantage of psychological testing that we are able to establish that this sort of incapacity for intense concentration appears in these people even where their intellectual endowments otherwise would not lead one to expect it, that is, as measured by other kinds of problem or other indexes. Many times, in connection with the mathematics problems presented on an intelligence test, hysterical subjects are quite unable to reproduce the processes by which they arrived at their answers, and this may hold true even if the answers are correct. It is clear, in such cases, that the answers were not reached by sharp concentration on facts, steps toward solution, and articulated principles that could be described later, but were reached by what one calls "hunches."

Everyone has such hunches, relatively passive and impressionistic "inspirations"—although, in compulsive and paranoid people, as I have indicated, such experiences tend to be infrequent. But most people know, also, that hunches are quite likely to be wrong and are even more likely to be incomplete or insufficient. For the normal person, they are a part of thinking and sometimes a great help, noticed, as it were, then checked with sharper attention and more direct concentration, and, finally, used or passed over. But, for the hysterical person, the hunch or the impression is the final, conscious cognitive product. It is often observed that hysterical people are relatively lacking in intellectual curiosity, and it is clear that this style of cognition is not consistent with sustained intellectual curiosity. In intellectual matters, an impressionistic style—cognition comprised of hunches and quick, relatively passive impressions—will tend to stop at the obvious, that which is easily and relatively immediately seen.

The second manifestation of this style of cognition is impressionability. We know hysterical people to be highly suggestible —that is, easily influenced by another's opinion; by the pressure of real or imagined external expectations; by fads, current prejudices, and excitements; and the like. It is not difficult to see, however, that hysterical impressionability extends considerably beyond these matters. A mode of cognition or a type of awareness that is characterized by the relative absence of active, sharply focused attention or by incapacity for actively searching concentration must be, to that extent, susceptible to any transient or accidental influences that, for one reason or another, are impressive.

I have indicated that impressionistic cognition ordinarily stops at the obvious or at that which is immediately and easily seen and is not compatible with curiosity. The same impressionistic character of this style of cognition that makes for satisfaction with the obvious or immediately apparent also makes for great susceptibility to that which is vivid, striking, or forcefully presented. Hysterical attention, in other words, is easily captured. So, we see in these people not merely suggestibility, but also general distractibility. Their line of thought—again, in sharp contrast to the determinedly focused attention of the obsessive-compulsive—is easily interrupted by transient influences. They are very easily surprised. If one imagines only the cognitive aspect of the Billie Burke type of caricature of a hysterical woman and if one puts aside the affective contents that usually accompany it—the abrupt blushing and embarrassment, the sudden giggle, and the like—one gets a picture of this distractibility and the scatteredness of thinking and expression that goes along with it.

The third point that I would like to mention here concerning the hysterical mode of cognition is more a consequence of it than a direct manifestation. To put it most simply, hysterical people are often remarkably deficient in knowledge. That is to say, they are deficient in factual knowledge as distinct, for instance, from what one might call knowledge of how to do. I am referring here not merely to the well-known naïveté of these people regarding sexual knowledge or other knowledge that might be considered highly charged emotionally. I mean, also, that they are deficient in knowledge in areas that are, as far as we have any right to assume, emotionally quite neutral. This deficiency, in other words, is a general matter, by no means re-

stricted to areas of content that can reasonably be assumed to
have come under repressive influence.

Again, psychological test data are of particular value in assess-
ing such a tendency, having the advantages of sampling neutral
material—for example, vocabulary and general information—
and of offering the means for comparing the level of this knowledge with the level of other aspects of intellectual capacity.
Deficiency in general factual information is a relatively reliable
diagnostic indicator of hysterical makeup; it appears regularly in
hysterical people. How could it be otherwise? Cognition of this
sort does not accumulate facts; instead, it accumulates impressions (such as the patient's "wham-bang" impression of her father) that, one may imagine, easily displace one another and
easily fuse with one another in memory and thus lose further in
distinctness and factual sharpness. Nor is this cognitive mode
likely to produce sustained intellectual interests or intense curiosity. Our experience suggests that hysterics are rare among sci-
entists and scholars, and we may suspect that they are headline
readers of newspapers. So the factual world of the hysterical person is probably thin and depleted. We will consider, in the next
section, the romance and fantasy that substitutes for facts and
knowledge in the hysterical person's subjective world.

I have mentioned these three features—the relative absence
of active concentration, the susceptibility to transient, impressive influences, and the relatively nonfactual subjective world of
the hysteric—in order to clarify and extend the picture of hysterical thinking and cognition and in order to indicate a form of
functioning that can give rise both to the specific operation of
repression and to certain other familiar hysterical characteristics
as well. Repression may be facilitated by this style in two ways.
First, the original cognition is not sharply, factually defined and
is not likely to be logically coordinated with other facts—for
example, names, dates, places, and so forth—but is impressionistic—for example, "Oh! He's wonderful!"—and highly susceptible to displacement by or fusion with other previous or subse-

quent impressions. Second, the relative incapacity for sharply focused attention and concentration and the passive, impressionistic, distractible nature of the cognitive style may be assumed to hold for the recollection process also and to make clear, sharp, factual recollection unlikely under the best of circumstances. These two factors, therefore, work in the same direction.

I am not saying that these factors *are* repression; I am saying that this mode of functioning or, specifically, of cognition decidedly favors the phenomenon we describe as "repression." In fact, given such a mode of functioning, clear, detailed, factual recollection of contents that are highly charged emotionally is hardly imaginable. In the case of the obsessive-compulsive, on the other hand, the affective tone of content is much less likely to impair such recollection.

It may be added that the striking inhibition of cognition, the not seeing of things that may be obvious to others or, as we sometimes describe it, the naïveté of hysterical people, is also understandable in the light of this cognitive style. Not seeing a highly and uncomfortably charged fact or, more accurately, not bringing into clear, sharp focus of attention that which may be dimly or peripherally experienced as uncomfortable is facilitated by the general absence of sharp focus of attention. Thus, one sometimes has the experience with a hysterical patient of noticing hints or suggestions of an unpleasant fact or possibility woven so conspicuously through the background of what the patient is saying that one finds it difficult to believe that the patient herself is unaware of it. But, in actual fact, she very often is, and it is exactly that failure to bring such a thought content, which is, as it were, on the periphery of attention, into sharp focus of attention that is facilitated by this style.

Hysterical Romance and Fantasy

If it can be said that the subjective world of the hysterical person is not quite an objective, factual one, it can be added, as I have already suggested, that it is instead a romantic and sentimental one. However, it is not altogether accurate to describe hysterical people as generally preoccupied with romantic fantasies. As a matter of fact, it often turns out that their "fantasy life" is rather meager. When we speak of hysterical romanticism, we mean, I believe, not merely time spent in romantic daydreams, but rather an outlook, a romantic attitude, that permeates everyday ideas and judgments.

Hysterical people, we know, are inclined to a Prince-Charming-will-come-and-everything-will-turn-out-all-right view of life, to nostalgic and idealized recollection of past figures and places, and to a sentimental view of the present. Nostalgic or idealized recollection, leaving aside once again its specific content, has exactly the sort of impressionistic quality that I have described. Typically, it is conspicuously lacking in factual detail, and, indeed, one sometimes has the impression that objective facts or factual details would spoil the story.

The same quality, of course, is evident in the hysterical person's idealization of the partner or object of romantic love; obliviousness to objective flaws or defects, which is generally an important part of romantic love, comes easily to hysterical people. It should be added, however, that immediate, global impressions of revulsion and disgust also come easily and with exactly the same obliviousness to complicating details. The hysterical-romantic view, thus, has its villains as well as its heroes. The hysterical patient who instantly idealizes a man whom she meets is likely to be just as quickly and wholly repelled by another—for example, a man with some physical deformity or unattractiveness—or frightened and intimidated by a third. This romantic outlook is not tied to any specific content, although certain contents are more suited to it than others. It only tends in general to be lacking in figures or recollections that contain the complications and contradictions that are usually the marks of real life.

If one asks what contents or what aspects of the world are likely to predominate in the mental life of a person who sees things in the impressionistic way I have described, the answer must be the vivid, the colorful, the emotionally charged, and the emotionally provocative. These are the things a hysterical person notices in the world, and they are the ingredients of romantic thought content. Some people search for things in the world— the compulsive person for technical data, the paranoid person, even more sharply, for clues—while others, hysterics among them, do not search, but are struck by things; and what these people see are the immediately striking, vivid, and colorful things in life. By the same token, the simple factual details, the less obvious aspects, the contradictions, and the dry, neutral weights and measurements of things tend to be absent from hysterical notice. The subjective world that emerges in this process is a colorful, exciting one, but it is often lacking in a sense of substance and fact.

A hysterical patient, for example, sees the therapist's office as a place of mystery and somewhat dark intrigue ("spooky")—this from the moment of first crossing the threshold and being impressed by the double doors, the relative quiet, and the big leather chairs. Only many months later does she begin to take a good look at the other, quite ordinary items of furniture in the room, the pictures on the wall, the condition of the carpet, and the like—all the things that make the room quite unmysterious.

I would like to consider now another hysterical trait that is closely related to the romantic attitude. This is the theatrical or play-acting quality that is often conspicuous in hysterical behavior. When we think of the histrionics of hysterical people, we may think also of their emotionality, but it is not emotionality as such that distinguishes theatrical behavior. It is, rather, the exaggerated or unconvincing quality of the emotionality (as, for example, when a quite hysterical man describes, with elaborate gestures and a false dramatic voice, the "pain and torment" he is going through at the hands of his girl friend). Yet, as flagrant as the play-acting or dramatic exaggerations of hysterical people may sometimes be, these people do not seem simply insincere. They do not seem, in other words, to be exaggerating or dramatizing their feelings in a conscious effort to accomplish some clear aim or produce some specific effect. The fact is that they are not clearly aware that they are acting at all. If it is suggested to a hysterical person, after a particularly impressive piece of histrionics that the feelings he is trying to portray do not seem entirely authentic or, perhaps, that he does not seem, himself, to believe completely in what he is saying, he is likely to become, not angry that the act has failed, but genuinely surprised, taken aback, somewhat confused and flustered. The capacity of hysterical people to become so ungenuine without being aware that they are so, is quite striking, and it seems to reflect the nature of their relationship to reality and to matters of fact in general. Let me explain.

It seems that the hysteric's romantic, fantastical, nonfactual, and insubstantial experience of the world also extends to his experience of his own self. He does not feel like a very substantial being with a real and factual history. Indeed, he is often hardly aware of his history, and, to the extent that he is, it is usually in the form of a romance-history, populated by impressionistically perceived, romantic, or idealized figures. He seems to feel like a character in this romance, a Cinderella or a heroic and dashing Don Juan. When we see hysterical histrionics, we can easily get the impression that the person is "carried away" by his own theatrics, and, I believe, there is a certain truth in this idea. He does not seem rooted in a sense of his factual being and history, in firm convictions, and a sense of the factual, objective world. Instead, he is actually "carried away" by the immediacy of his responses to and the ease with which his whole awareness is captured by vivid impressions, romantic provocations, transient moods of his own, or the fantasy characters that, for whatever reason, appeal to him. He is "off," then, on a feeling that does not run deep, but is not completely absent.

I have sometimes had the experience, and I imagine other therapists share it, of being with a hysterical patient and, as she talked in an animated and somewhat scattered and diffuse way —now about this disappointment, now about that funny thing that happened, now about the exciting man she had just met— of thinking to myself that I really did not know just how she felt or what her mood "really" was. On several occasions, I have mentioned this impression to the patient and have received, in response, an interesting kind of confirmation. The literal response, given quite cheerfully, was, "I don't know what I *really* feel like." But these patients seem to mean, further, "I don't know what I *am* like." They seem to feel as if they were virtually weightless and floating,[5] attracted here, repelled there, captivated first by this and then by that. They seem to be without that sense of personal substance and definiteness for which one prerequisite at least must be a greater independence from or resistance to impressive but transient influences. The hysterical person's emotional behavior or ideas do not seem to the observer to be anchored in a real and deep interest, a long history, or an abiding purpose, and, in fact, they are not. We will return to this subject later.

There is one other aspect of the hysterical person's relationship to reality that can be described in terms of an expression that children use when they play games that involve winning or losing objects of value. They say, "Let's play 'for keeps,' " or "Let's play 'for fun.' " This distinction has nothing to do with

---

[5] Incidentally, those familiar with the Rorschach will know how frequently images—one can confidently say self-images—of wispy, floating things appear in hysterical Rorschach records.

the rules of the game or activity proper, and therefore does not necessarily influence the behavior of the participants in any way that would be obvious to an observer. It has to do only with the question of whether the results of the game will have material consequences and, therefore, with the participants' feelings about the game. "For real," in contrast to "for fun," means that this game *counts* and is regarded as a serious matter. When one observes hysterical people closely, their behavior sometimes indicates a certain loss of a sense that things "count," on occasions or in circumstances when others might regard the given event as a quite serious matter. This feature of hysterical subjective experience seems, certainly, related to the impressionistic, nonfactual, and fantastical subjective world that I have described, but it deserves some special attention.

This attitude becomes apparent, sometimes, in the form of astonishment or incredulity on the part of hysterical people when a consequence of some action of their own or of circumstances of which they were aware comes to pass, a consequence that may have been completely predictable to everyone else.

One patient, approaching middle age and married to a man many years her junior, becomes aware that her husband shows obvious and increasing signs of discontent with the marriage. She, thinking to pacify him, suggests psychotherapy. He accepts her suggestion, but shortly afterward announces that he wants a divorce. She is astonished.

Another hysterical patient, a woman in her late twenties, is not enthusiastic when her sister, known to the patient to be an alcoholic and promiscuous, asks if she may move into the patient's house for a short time. Some years before, during a previous marriage of the patient's, the sister had seduced her husband, an event that contributed to the breakup of the marriage. Although the patient considers, on this occasion, the possibility of a similar turn of events, she does not consider it a "serious possibility" and agrees to her sister's request. But the same thing does happen with the present husband, and when the patient discovers it—some time after most people's suspicions would have been aroused—she is amazed. She says, "You know . . . I did actually think of this possibility . . . the thought did occur to me . . . but I never thought it would *really happen*."

A third patient, a thirty-year-old woman, has periodic stormy, hysterical outbursts of anger directed principally at her husband. On one occasion, she is astonished that he tells her that he cannot put up with it. "He really means it," she says in amazement and adds, "But I don't really mean the things I say."

These people, if they had asked themselves certain questions sharply and seriously, would very likely have come up with the right answers, that is, they would have predicted these events or, at least, their reasonable probability. But they did not ask themselves these questions sharply and seriously. Of course, it is true that they may have had motives for avoiding the answers, but a motive for a distortion of reality is never sufficient explanation for its accomplishment. It is their diffuse, impressionistic experience of the world—the general absence of a sharp look at, and a clear sense of, plain hard fact—that makes possible the avoidance of these serious questions.

Other people, certainly including normal people, also have such experiences as those I have described. Other people say, when surprised at a turn of events, "Now, I thought of that, but I just didn't think it would really happen," and it occurs also with patients who are not exceedingly hysterical that, if a remark of the therapist's brings something abruptly into sharp focus, they will first react with surprise and then, a few moments later, comment, "But I knew it all along." But, for the hysterical person this seems to be the general rule. Real facts and real consequences of real facts are seen only dimly, peripherally; they are not substantial or sharp until events or someone else forcefully says, "Look!"

The feeling that things don't really count or, to put it more accurately, the absence of the feeling that they *do* count, is most visible when it is interrupted or sharply contradicted by the force of circumstances, but it exists as a continuous, general feeling and is an aspect of many of the typical attitudes of hysterical people. It is evident sometimes, for example, in the disinclination they may show toward the hard facts of money. In more impulsive hysterics, given to impetuous romance and infatuations, it is sometimes very much in the background of the feeling that nothing is important but we two. Possibly, it is one of the reasons why aging so often comes as a sudden shock to these people. It is very much a part of what is often described as hysterical immaturity and the wide-eyed, innocent quality of many hysterics. It is, perhaps, even an aspect of a certain cultural image of femininity, now somewhat out of date except, perhaps, among some classes of Southern women. Certainly, it is closely related to hysterical naïveté, but it is distinguishable from the sheer factual naïveté that is also evident in these people. It is an attitude toward reality rather than an ignorance of it. Rather than attribute it to repressive tendencies, therefore, we shall attribute both tendencies to a more general mode of cognition and subjective experience.

This attitude toward reality has one other interesting manifestation that is quite familiar to psychiatry. It has often been remarked that hysterics are capable of regarding their symptoms, for example, conversion symptoms, with curious dispassion or indifference, *la belle indifférence*, as it was called in the days of descriptive psychiatry. One does not hear this phrase very much anymore, possibly because dramatic conversion symptoms are not seen so frequently. However, the attitude of indifference— or, as I would say, the attitude that it doesn't really count—is still to be found.

Hysterical Emotions

There is an interesting paradox involved in hysterical emotionality. If it is true, as we have seen, that an air of fantasy pervades the hysterical person's mental life and a sense of insubstantiality and indefiniteness characterizes both his experience of the external world and his experience of himself, how is it possible that the hysterical person is also characterized by vivid, intense emotions? One would think that vivid emotional life, strong feelings, would above all guarantee an equally vivid, sharp sense of oneself, but, in this case, it certainly does not have that result. It is well to keep this paradox in mind as we take a closer look at hysterical emotionality. I would like to approach that subject at its extreme point—the hysterical emotional outburst.

Emotional outbursts or explosions are sometimes the major complaint that brings these people to treatment, although the actual complaint may be as much or more that of the husband or other relative who is the object of the outbursts as the patient's. It is noticeable in fact that, aside from a brief period of contrition after each episode, the patient is often rather unperturbed by the symptom. Probably, most often, these are angry outbursts, but they may be mingled with depressive feelings.

One typical patient, for example, a twenty-six-year-old woman, would frequently have such an outburst after going out with her fiancé. The beginning of the evening would go quietly enough as a rule, but, on the way home in the car, she would begin, at first in a tense but still controlled way, to criticize some piece of his behavior, perhaps a slight inconsideration of her that, she felt, he had been guilty of during the evening. She was quite ready to acknowledge later and was dimly aware even at the time that the specific subject that she chose for her irritation was a trivial one in almost all cases. At any rate, within a few minutes, whether her fiancé chose to defend his behavior or apologize for it, her anger would grow, she would hurl accusations at him, and ultimately scream, sob, grab something that was at hand and throw it or threaten him with it. The outburst would subside shortly into an angry sulking and would usually be terminated only when, still sulking, she would leave him.

During these outbursts, no matter what the original provocation, the content of her attacks was approximately the same. She simply hurled at him those accusations that she imagined would hurt him the most. Thus, she accused him of being selfish, insensitive, stingy.

and the like. However, here again I would like to consider not so much the specific content of such outbursts, which is quite variable from patient to patient and from occasion to occasion, but rather their general form, which is not so variable.

I have already suggested that the attitude that is sometimes described as indifference on the part of the hysteric toward her symptoms is, to some extent, manifest also in her attitude toward these emotional outbursts. I would like to return to that fact and consider it more carefully, because the reactions after such an outburst and, in general, the retrospective attitude seem to me, not peripheral to the symptom proper, but an essential and quite revealing part of it. If the hysteric's relative indifference to and detachment from conversion symptoms is noteworthy, the same reaction to her own emotional explosions is certainly more so. Conversion symptoms, after all, remain rather mysterious and perhaps somewhat ephemeral matters. In the case of one's own emotional feelings and responses, however, and such vivid ones at that, a sense of detachment seems more difficult to understand. Yet, I believe that observation will show that hysterical people do, in fact, regard their own emotional outbursts very much as they might regard conversion symptoms; that is, they do not quite regard the content of their outbursts as something they have really felt, but rather as something that has been visited on them or, as it were, something that has passed through them.

In the case that I have referred to, the patient spoke of the explosive episode in a manner that would suggest, except for certain details, that she had hardly been present. One or two days, it is true, were full of expressions of contrition and regret, but this period passed quickly, and even these expressions, on close examination, already contained hints of the detachment that shortly became more obvious. Even during these first few days, when the episode was referred to with tears and genuine concern about her fiancé's feelings, she spoke of it—and this is the remarkable feature—with virtually no sense that it represented her feelings. It was not only that this quite intelligent woman failed to notice, a few days after the event, that those angry feelings, which appeared with such intensity then, might not be altogether absent now, although that in itself would be noteworthy. Beyond that, however, she clearly did not regard the feelings that she had expressed during the outburst as representing what she actually felt toward her fiancé, even at that time. On the contrary, she referred to it, whether during the period of regret immediately afterwards or later, as a mysterious thing, something akin to a seizure, a strange passion that had got her in its grip; in short, it was not something that she felt. "But I don't mean it," she said with puzzlement, and, if her puzzlement was somewhat underscored, it did not seem insincere. And, she added, she did not mean it at the time. Quite the contrary, she said, she loves her fiancé and, furthermore respects him. And she did, in fact, say this in a way that was entirely believable and convincing.

Sometimes, these patients attribute their outbursts or, as they regard them, seizures to menstrual periods, and this woman had abandoned this theory only reluctantly and then not completely, despite the fact that there was no evident coincidence of dates. Another patient with similar symptoms, who had been initiated by reading into the mysteries of psychoanalysis, turned, after other theories failed to account for her outbursts, to her own history and her "unconscious." "Why? Why? I say things that I don't mean at all. I don't know why. . . . Maybe my brother—I always felt rejected by him. But I don't remember feeling angry at him. Hurt, maybe, but. . . ."

One should not be misled on this point; this search for a "cause" for the emotional outbursts in childhood or the unconscious is not simply a search for insight. It restates in one way or another, explicitly or by implication, the patient's claim that these outbursts do not represent what she feels or felt, but represent an alien force (the "unconscious") that takes possession of her. This is a defensive claim, to be sure. The patient offers, in effect, a plea of temporary insanity, and her search is for a causal or provoking agent that will support this plea. But there is no doubt that, although she makes this plea for defensive reasons, she *can* make it because it reflects her actual experience. In fact, as one realizes the extent of this experience—"these were not my feelings"—one can hardly avoid recalling another, quite famous type of hysterical symptom, namely, the cases of so-called multiple personality, in which even the memory of the Mr. Hyde-like thoughts and behavior of one period is completely lost to consciousness afterwards.

In considering these emotional outbursts, it is important to note one other, more general feature of the behavior and emotional life of hysterical patients. They are, in their regular behavior, usually quite mild-mannered. The patient first cited, for example, considered herself a "decent" person and in fact was so, and her regretful puzzlement after her outbursts always conveyed such a feeling as, "How is it possible that I, a nice and decent person, should be doing these things?" Notwithstanding the angry outbursts, she was otherwise somewhat inhibited and, for example, was usually quite uncomfortable about making what probably would have been for someone else a mild, rather trivial aggressive assertion. Behavior of an assertive, mildly aggressive, or demanding sort seemed to her "rude" or "nasty." Although she felt that she was primarily concerned about hurting other people's feelings in this connection, there is no doubt that, for the most part, it was she and not the other who could not tolerate "unpleasantness." Yet, some of the very people whom she ordinarily treated in this rather gingerly fashion might, at one time or another, be the object of a full-fledged outburst of anger.

This combination of affective explosions and inhibition of nonexplosive affect and behavior is typical of these people, and parallels to it can be found in other emotional areas. It is well known, for instance, that some more impulsive hysterical women, although frequently given to sudden, almost explosively emotional infatuations, are nevertheless inhibited in sustained and less explosive love.

How can we understand all this? Is it enough to say, as sometimes is said, that the hysterical person's affect is shallow, ephemeral, and transient rather than deep and sustained? The description sounds plausible, in general—at least, if one stretches a point and accepts the quality of such angry outbursts within the compass of "shallow" affect. It may easily be that, if we objectively describe her emotions as "shallow," we refer to what the patient experiences subjectively when she says, "I didn't really feel that way at all." But this does not, I think, advance our understanding of hysterical emotion much further, nor, particularly, our understanding of the relationship of this sort of affect to other aspects of hysterical functioning.

Let us recall at this point something of what has been said about the cognitive functioning of hysterical people and about their subjective experience in general. I have described their cognition as impressionistic, relatively immediate, and global. The cognitive experience of the hysteric is an experience not of sharply observed facts and developed judgments, but of quick hunches and impressions. In line with this, these are people whose attention is relatively easily captured and who are suggestible and easily carried away by that which is impressive or strikes an immediate chord. Accordingly, their judgments are labile; they are not—and are not experienced as being—rooted in firm convictions, really thought through, or clearly based on knowledge or the facts of personal experience. In the sense that their judgments and ideas are not deeply integrated products, but are quick, labile ones highly influenced by transient impressions, it may be said that these judgments and ideas are not truly or, at least, not thoroughly representative of them and do not feel so. I would like to suggest now that the emotional outbursts of the hysteric, the abrupt discharges of affect that subside quickly and are experienced later as though they had passed through their subject without her real participation, are consist-

ent with this style of functioning and could exist only in the
context of such a style.

How does a half-conscious, half-formed impulse or feeling-
sensation normally become transformed into an articulated,
fully conscious emotion? Some kind of integrative process must
be involved through which that half-formed feeling becomes
associatively connected to and organized with existing attitudes,
feelings, interests, and the like, and thereby accrues associative
content, gains in weight so to speak, and gains in articulation
and refinement at the same time. Now let us imagine that the
hysteric is characterized by a general immediacy of subjective
experience, including not only cognitive experience, but also
affective experience. The relative absence of complex cognitive
integration—the quick, impressionistic cognition, in other words
—will have a parallel in the immediacy and peremptoriness of
affect. This affect, easily triggered or excited, abruptly emerges
into consciousness as the final affective product, just as the immediate, global impression emerges as the final cognitive product. In general, in other words, it appears that these people are
characterized by a too-quick and insufficient organization, refinement, and integration of mental contents. The normal integrative mental processes through which, we may imagine, a half-
conscious hunch becomes a conscious judgment, a half-formed
and diffuse impression becomes a clear idea, and a half-conscious
and immediate feeling-sensation becomes an articulated and
deep emotion; these processes are, in the hysterical person, markedly attenuated.

An emotion that emerges into consciousness as a result of a
normal process of integration and associative connection of a
half-formed and immediate impulse or feeling with existing interests or aims and other sentiments and tastes—such an emotion feels like one's own; it is consistent with one's self, and it
feels deep. But this integrative development does not occur in
hysterical people, no more in the affective than in the cognitive
sphere, and, in this sense, their experience of not quite partici-

pating in their own emotional outburst is an experience of an actual fact; in this sense, their emotions actually do not fully represent them. This insufficiency of integrative processes and development causes their affects to be explosive, abrupt, and labile, on the one hand, and relatively undifferentiated, gross, and black or white, on the other. To put it another way, the hysterical affect, like the cognition, does not emerge as a well-developed and articulated mental content in a clearly focused, well-differentiated awareness, but immediately dominates and captures a diffuse and passive awareness.

There are many hysterical people, women particularly, who are not necessarily characterized by specific outbursts or explosions of affect, but who are instead characterized by more or less continuous outbursts that are perhaps just below the level of intensity of the explosions we have been considering. In these people, one can see very much the same mode of functioning at work. In one of his novels, Henry James has one character describe another as follows: "She rattled this off with the air of a woman who had the reputation of saying everything that came into her head, and with a strong French accent." [6] I would add that this hysterical woman said "everything that came into her head" exactly because everything that would, for another person, have been a half-formed whim, a fancy, a transient impression, or a momentary emotion, did, in fact, at that moment dominate her mind. In the presence of such a person, one does have a feeling that the whole person is not participating in these affects and expressions. We know and expect that the next day such a person is likely to have forgotten half of what she experienced and feel about much of the other half that she "didn't really mean it." This, I believe, is what we mean to describe when we call hysterical emotions "shallow."

The same mode of functioning that produces affects of this

---

[6] Henry James, *The American* in *Four Selected Novels of Henry James* (New York: The Universal Library, 1946), p. 72.

quality, in general, produces large quantities of them. Emotion, particularly emotion of this labile sort, is, by its nature, a relatively immediate type of experience and does not necessarily require for its basic existence a great degree of psychological integrative activity. This is certainly not to say that affects do not reflect or are independent of the development of psychological integrative capacities, but only to say that affects, as such, may and do exist when such development is not exceedingly great. The emotions of childhood, in general, may be less subtle than those of adulthood, but they could certainly not be called less present or less vivid. One consequence of this is that, within certain important limits that we will consider further in the following chapter, a psychological organization in which mental contents appear in an immediate, impressionistic way is likely to be characterized, on the one hand, by "shallowness" and peremptoriness of affect and, on the other hand, by a great deal of such affect.

We have referred, also, to the fact that hysterical people, highly emotional as they tend to be, are nevertheless usually quite inhibited in certain respects, and we are now in a better position to understand this. It is apparent that the sort of emotional experience described—explosive and vivid but ephemeral and not "deeply" experienced—is consistent with the romantic and insubstantial experience these people seem to have of the world and of themselves. This is the subjective world that is the product of the hysterical style, and it is a world in which they may live comparatively comfortably. A "serious" emotion, on the other hand, an emotion that counts and is felt with a deep sense of "meaning it," is, like a serious conviction, altogether at odds with this subjective world, and is extremely discomforting to the hysteric. These people feel like lightweights, and when it happens—and since human beings do not function with the perfect consistency of machinery, it does happen—that they feel something more substantial, whether that is an emotion or a judgment, they unmistakably shrink from it. This holds true over a great range of specific emotional or ideational contents. Thus, the most sentimental hysteric will often be inhibited in love and would not think of having a political conviction.

Hysterical people are by no means the only ones whose cognition and subjective experience are characterized by impressionistic, quickly and insufficiently organized mental contents, nor by any means the most severely or conspicuously so. As I shall try to show in the next chapter, those individuals who are described as passive or impulsive characters exhibit these features in even more marked degree without, however, being characterized by great emotionality in the usual sense of that word. They are inclined, rather, to impulsive action, that is, action that seems to others and feels to them not entirely deliberate, not wholly participated in or decided upon.

Impulsive Styles

The group of styles to be considered here does not altogether coincide with any one psychiatric diagnosis. In one case, impulsive behavior may be considered a primary feature of the diagnosis whereas, in another case, perhaps closely similar from the standpoint of style of functioning, some other psychiatric feature or symptom will dominate the diagnosis. Thus, the group to be discussed includes most of those persons usually diagnosed as impulsive characters or psychopathic characters, some of those who are called passive-neurotic characters and narcissistic characters, and certain kinds of male homosexuals, alcoholics, and probably addicts.

This group, despite its apparent diversity, has a general mode of action in common, although it must be added that a number of variants can be identified within this general mode. It also has in common other essential features associated with this mode of action—a style of cognition and, of particular interest, a characteristic and distinctive type of subjective experience of action and motivation to action.

The distinctive quality of this subjective experience revolves around an impairment of normal feelings of deliberateness and intention. It is manifested in the nature of the experience, for these people, of "impulse" or "irresistible impulse" and in the significance of "whim" in their mental lives. The subjective experience of impulse is not as simple a matter as it might at first seem. Sometimes, the quality of that experience, together with the relatively primitive nature of some impulsive actions, has led to the view that impulsive actions must be actual eruptions in which regular executive apparatuses or generally operative modes of functioning are by-passed or broken through. My conclusion will be different, namely, that the subjective experience of impulse is itself an aspect of a style of functioning.

A few words should be added here to explain why I have included certain conditions usually described as "passive" among the varieties of impulsive styles. The reason is that examination of the formal qualities of the two sorts of condition—that marked by impulsiveness and that marked by extreme passivity —shows them to be very closely related. In fact, I believe it would be in keeping with the formal similarity of the two sorts of condition to speak of a general passive-impulsive style. Certainly, there are conditions in which the symptomatic behavior could just as well be placed in the one category as the other. Not all impulsive action is vivid or dramatic. Sometimes, action that is very quiet and descriptively very passive, such as the drinking of an alcoholic, may, in its formal features, be indistinguishable from an action that is much more vivid and, therefore, more conspicuously impulsive. I will try to show, also, that, in extremely passive or "weak" people, the characteristic subjective experience of their own actions, in particular the experience of "giving in" to external pressure or temptation, is closely related to the subjective experience of the more typical impulsive character.

The Subjective Experience of "Impulse"

An impulsive patient, an artist, spoke about a recent action of his, a gambling binge, in the following way: "I just *did* it—I don't know why." What does he mean by this?

This patient probably means to say, "I didn't really mean to do it," or "I didn't intend to do it." Some such statement as, "I just *did* it—I don't know why," is often made by impulsive people, sometimes regretfully and guiltily and sometimes not. It is true that such statements, like the hysteric's disavowal of her emotional outbursts, are not always entirely genuine. That is, they often contain not just a communication of subjective experience, but also a plea—in this case, something like the plea for the defense, "Guilty but without premeditation."

Nevertheless, although the point may be exaggerated for defensive reasons, such expressions do seem to reflect a subjective experience of a remarkable sort, one that is in certain respects similar to the hysteric's experience of emotional outbursts, but is by no means identical with it. It is an experience of having executed a significant action, not a trivial one, without a clear and complete sense of motivation, decision, or sustained wish. It is an experience of an action, in other words, that does not feel completely deliberate or fully intended. Yet, these are not experiences of external compulsion or of submission to moral principle. They are experiences of wanting, of wish, or even of decision; but they are experiences of exceedingly abrupt, transient, and partial wish, wish that is so attenuated as to be hardly comparable to the normal experience of wanting or deciding and so attenuated as to make possible or even plausible a plea of, "Guilty but without premeditation." The experience seems, in some respects, to approximate the normal experience of whim.

Such an attenuated motivation experience takes a variety of forms in impulsive and passive-impulsive people. Sometimes, the experience seems virtually identical with the normal experience of whim, except, of course, that the "whim" may in this case involve much more consequential action than normal whim does. Thus, the psychopath might say, "I just felt like it," meaning that the whim struck him at the moment, in explanation of a robbery. Another variety of this general type of subjective experience is the experience of "urge" or "impulse." That is, the experience of urge or impulse is not, from this point of view, a detached perception of an actual seizure that overrides what one wants to do, but rather is a distortion and attenuation of the normal experience of wanting in which the sense of active intention and deliberateness is especially impaired and, usually, even further disavowed for defensive reasons. This understanding suggests that the typical statement of an irresistible impulse—"I don't want to do it, but I just can't control my impulse"—may usually be translated as, "I don't feel I ought to do it, and I would shrink from doing it deliberately, but, if, quickly and while I am not looking, my feet, my hands, or my impulses just *do* it, I can hardly be blamed."

In other cases, essentially the same type of attenuated, nondeliberate motivation experience is described, again, we may assume, with defensive exaggeration, as a virtually reflexive response to an external provocation or opportunity—"I didn't mean to do it, but then I saw the money lying there on the table, and somehow I just took it." Among the passive-impulsive, "weak" characters that we will consider later, still another type of reflex-like response is described—"I didn't really want to do it, but he pressed, and somehow I just gave in." These varieties of experience—whim, urge or impulse, and giving in—are essentially similar from the standpoint of their formal qualities. All of them describe a distortion and attenuation of normal motivation experience of the same sort. All are abrupt, transient, and partial experiences of wanting, choosing, or deciding—experiences of action in which the sense of active intention and deliberateness is markedly impaired.

I have already alluded to the fact that this mode of experience forms a basis for, that is, facilitates, certain defensive operations that are well known in impulsive characters. More specifically, the actual impairment of the sense of intention and deliberateness forms a basis for the defensive disavowal of personal responsibility, to others and to the subject himself. Perhaps, the best known of such defensive operations is that of "externalization of responsibility."

For example, a burglar explains his repeated offenses as follows. "It seems like every time I came out [of prison], instead of having someone to help me, there was always some guy to stick a crowbar in my hands." [1]

This man says, in effect, that he never really intends to do it; he is just weak and gives in. Another sort of externalization of responsibility is represented in the claim of irresistible temptation, for example, ". . . the money was just lying there. . . ." Here, also, the plea is, in effect, "I didn't really intend to do it." These externalizations of responsibility are, then, virtual equivalents of the defensive plea of uncontrollable impulse, for this states also, "I did it, but I didn't really intend to do it." All such disavowals of responsibility may, in other words, be expected in impulsive or passive-impulsive people, whenever a defensive need for them arises, because they have a basis in an aspect of the actual subjective experience characteristic of these people.

Subjective experience of whim or impulse is obviously not limited to impulsive characters, but is a part of the mental life of all people.[2] But, in the case of the impulsive style, this mode of motivation experience is predominant and occupies psychological areas that normally would be occupied by experience of more active and sustained wanting, choosing, or deciding. In this sense it can be called a distortion of normal subjective experience. The nature of this mode of experience in impulsive people is, I shall try to show, consistent with other aspects of their style of functioning and, specifically, follows from a general deficiency

---

[1] William Krasner, "Hoodlum Priest and Respectable Convicts," *Harper's Magazine*, 222 (February 1961), p. 62.

[2] But it is sometimes drastically curtailed—for example, in obsessive-compulsives and paranoid people.

of active organizing and integrative mental functions. The experience of impulse, therefore, is not occasional, but regular in these people; and it does not occur as a result of the breakdown of executive functions, but is an integral part of their existing form. Some subjective sense of estrangement from motivating desires or the actions that follow from them is a regular feature of this attenuated experience of motive, just as the normal person does not feel wholly identified with every passing whim of his.

This mode of motivation experience, with its sense of nondeliberateness, is a vital element in many other features of this style of functioning and in many of the commonly recognized traits of impulsive people. For example, it obviously is consistent with and facilitates speedy action, even in persons whose conscience might not permit such action to be executed intentionally. Probably, also, the sense of nondeliberateness is a vital element in one of the most interesting traits—almost unique among the neuroses—of many impulsive characters: their apparent self-confidence and freedom from inhibition and anxiety.[3] Certainly, to mention a commonplace parallel, it is well known that many normal people feel increased freedom from inhibition and increased self-confidence when they are intoxicated and, as we say, "don't quite know what they are doing."

The Quality of Impulsive Action

If we consider the formal characteristics of impulsive action, certain ones easily come to mind. For example, I have mentioned that impulsive action is speedy; it is typically quick in

---

[3] This trait is, to some extent, exhibited in only one other pathological condition, as far as I am aware—the hypomanic. In this and a number of other connections, there are significant formal relationships between hypomanic and impulsive conditions. A relationship of a different sort between the two is already known to psychoanalysis. See, Otto Fenichel, *The Psychoanalytic Theory of Neurosis* (New York: Norton, 1945), p. 410.

execution, and, more important, it is speedy in the sense that the period between thought and execution is usually short. To mention another, it is usually abrupt or discontinuous in contrast to normal activity, which ordinarily seems to follow from avowed or at least perceptible aims or visible preparations. To these two characteristics, we may add a third, perhaps more basic one. Impulsive action is action that is unplanned. This is not to say that it is necessarily unanticipated; the drinker may very well anticipate his next binge. But anticipation, such as anticipation of the next snowfall, is by no means the same as planning.[4] Each of these characteristics—speediness, abruptness, and lack of planning—seems to reflect a deficiency in certain mental processes that are normally involved in the translation of incipient motives into actions. The translation here of motive or inclination into action seems to "short-circuit"[5] certain active mental processes. What are these processes? May we attribute to the deficiency or "short-circuiting" of them the impairment of subjective sense of deliberateness and intention that also characterizes these people?

In the normal person, the whim or the half-formed inclination to do something is the beginning of a complex process, although, if all is well, it is a smooth and automatic one. The whim, first of all, appears in a context of relatively stable and continuous interests and aims. In this context, it gains significance or loses it, commands and receives further attention or not. If it does command attention—if it is interesting, appealing, or exciting, in other words—it influences to one degree or another the previously existing direction of interest, and, in turn,

---

[4] Actually, the description of impulsive action as unplanned must be qualified. It is planning in the long-term sense in which impulsive people are deficient. Short-term, practical planning seems to involve different processes and is, as I shall discuss later, often quite highly developed.

[5] This very descriptive term was used by David Rapaport in a similar connection. David Rapaport, Roy Schafer, and Merton Gill, *Diagnostic Psychological Testing*, Vol. II (Chicago: Yearbook Publishers, 1945).

it is very likely modified by that previously existing direction. Thus, the whim is organized or integrated into the fabric of current aims and interests. In fact, it is even somewhat arbitrary to consider the half-formed whim or inclination to be the beginning of this integrative process, since the shape and the very existence of that inclination is obviously in part a function of the previously existing level and direction of interests. The man who is interested in art will notice the gallery on his way to work and feel inclined to go in; one without such a previous interest may not even notice it. At any rate, in the course of the normal integrative process, a whim may either be dismissed or it may accrue interest and emotional and associative support from the existing fabric of aims and interests. Such a process, we may imagine, witnesses the transformation of a passively experienced whim (or impulse) into an experience of active, intended, and deliberate want, choice, or decision. What might otherwise have been a transient whim now becomes a sustained desire. With this, a basis is laid for planning, and, with planning, the sense of deliberateness is probably further consolidated.

This process of the integration of a whim with an organization of stable interests has various simultaneous results. First, it accomplishes the transformation of a half-formed whim or impulse into an active want and intention. Second, it accomplishes an actual modification and development of the content of the whim or impulse; the integration with existing interests and the accrual of associative contents and affects will change it, and, indeed, the active planning of a course of action will modify and develop the original wish even further. A third consequence of the integrative process is a change in attitude toward the object. As a half-formed whim accrues content and emotional support from existing interests, so must its object accrue additional dimensions of significance, actual and potential; as a whim is transformed into a clear and active intention, that intention must be accompanied by a heightened awareness of and interest in its external object. Thus, the difference between a passing whim to become a doctor and an intention, decision, or plan to become a doctor is not only a difference in the status or level of the wish, but also a difference in the awareness of the object.

If these are among the results of the normal integrative process, it can be added that a failure in each item is evident in the impulsive person, where the integrative process is "short-circuited." When a whim cannot accrue affective and associative support from stable and continuous aims and interests, it cannot develop into a sustained, active want, choice, or intention. It remains an impulse, lacking in a sense of intention, transient, and partial. When the content of a whim or impulse fails to be modified by stable aims or enriched and modulated by associative and affective connections in such an integrative process, that content remains primitive and bare, and, failing to be anchored in stable interests, it tends to shift erratically. Finally, the impulsive person, experiencing an urge where someone else experiences a more rich and sustained intention, can have only a very limited interest in or even awareness of the independent properties of the object of that urge. He does not have an interest in the object, but an interest in satisfaction.

I have described the insufficiency of similar integrative processes in hysterical people, but it is plain that, in comparison with these features of impulsive functioning, the labile affects of the hysteric are relatively well developed. Compare, for instance, the romantic interest of the hysteric in an object of infatuation—an interest that is certainly likely to be transient and that we may even call "shallow"—with the even more transient and essentially exploitative interest of many impulsive characters in a current sexual object.

Even if the evidence of some deficiency or "short-circuiting" of the integrative process is apparent, the further question remains: In what does this deficiency consist? To this, we may add the corollary question: What sort of integrative process *does* take place in impulsive people? For there can be no doubt that even the reckless, impulsive actions of which these people are capable are an outcome of some integrative process. The alternative possibility that these actions are simply eruptions of instinctual energy in which executive apparatuses and functions are inoperative would be difficult to support theoretically for any person, and, if such a thing occurs in anyone, it certainly is not in the case of nonpsychotic people. On the contrary, it is exactly the characteristic of impulsive people that neither are they helplessly immobilized by surges of instinctual energy nor do they explode chaotically. They *act*; and those impulsive actions that are, from one standpoint, so erratic and unmindful of consequences are nevertheless typically executed with perfectly adequate and, in many cases, even superb competency. We will return to this important fact later, but at present it stands as incontrovertible evidence that impulsive action is the outcome of an integrative process, although certainly a different one from the normal person's and decidedly a deficient one.

If we consider that the deficiency that I have referred to is a deficiency in the integration of a whim or impulse with a preexisting organization of stable and continuous aims and interests, we are confronted with a very important fact about impulsive people. Acquaintance with these people regularly reveals them to be remarkably lacking in active interests, aims, values, or goals much beyond the immediate concerns of their own lives. Durable emotional involvements—deep friendships or love—are not much in evidence. Family interests or even personal career goals are usually not very strong or occupying. These people usually do not even have abiding, long-range personal plans or ambitions, not to mention more abstract aims, purposes, or values. Typically, they are quite uninterested not only in cultural or intellectual matters, but also in ideological or political issues. Events of general public interest or concern—a threat of war, elections, and the like—usually pass them by with very little notice. There is one type of exception to this, a highly significant one, that I will indicate now only by an example but will return to later.

On a certain occasion, a patient of this sort who had seemed, until then, utterly uninterested in international affairs surprised his therapist by showing a keen, excited interest in some recent news. The headlines that day and the previous several days had concerned a new series of atomic bomb tests and had seemed quite ominous and threatening. He excitedly asked if the therapist had seen them. They had given him the idea—and he had already taken some steps —to go into a disaster and fallout supply kit business. He was now quite enthusiastic about its prospects.

If impulsive people are relatively lacking in aims, interests, goals, and values that extend beyond the most immediate concerns of their own lives, they are indeed lacking in essential equipment for the successful modulation and development of impulse or whim and for "resistance" to impulse or whim as well. Aims and interests such as these are by their nature relatively stable and continuous, and they are basic to the stability and continuity of living exactly because they are long-range and extend beyond transient and immediate needs and influences. On the other hand, interests that are restricted to the immediate needs and concerns of life, that is, to immediate gains and satisfactions, are necessarily labile and erratic. Long-range interests, values, and emotional involvements are the very structures that comprise the pre-existing, stable context within which a whim or impulse emerges for the normal person. This is the context that normally exercises a selective tendency upon the arousal of inclinations from the beginning, merely because of the direction of existing interests. This is the context from which a whim may accrue sustaining emotional and associative support, and the context that, at the same time, reshapes and modulates its content. For example, in a context of pre-existing attitudes of affection, readiness for intimacy, certain life anticipations, and the like, an immediate response to an attractive girl can develop, accrue content, and be sustained; the girl "clicks." Without this context, the experience must remain one of sexual impulse.

At the same time that such structures are essential to the development and modulation of an impulse, they also perform an essential stabilizing, I would even say conservative, function. Such structures stabilize against immediate, automatic, and indiscriminate translation into action of transient impulses or responses. When I say "stabilize against," I do not mean a state of being rigidly armored against or insensitive to passing whims or provocations. I mean only that a context of stable, long-range interests and values provides a viewpoint or perspective from which, so to speak, a whim is experienced as a whim, perhaps exciting, interesting, or at least worth it and perhaps not, rather than being experienced, immediately and automatically, as the only next thing to do. Thus, such structures, both in their impulse-developing and stabilizing functions, comprise an essential basis for deliberate activity.

This understanding, incidentally, can easily be applied to the concept of "tolerance" of frustration or tension and can serve, also, to correct certain unpsychological connotations of that concept. When psychologists speak of the low "tolerance" of impulsive people for frustration or for tension generally, they mean, I believe, the limited capacity of these people for forebearance. The concept seems to me to have at least a partially moral connotation.[6] Although the observation certainly has some descriptive validity, it does not take sufficient account of the fact that the same objective frustration is by no means identically experienced subjectively by different people.

The normal person "tolerates" frustration or postpones the satisfaction of his whim at least in part because he is also interested in other things; his heart is set on goals and interests that are independent of the immediate frustration or extend beyond

---

[6] It has a moral connotation in the sense of implying that (moral) will should somehow be able to rise above psychological necessity. I must admit, however, that I am not sure whether the concept of "tolerance" is generally understood in this sense or in the sense in which it is used in mechanical work, meaning "allowance."

the whim and supercede it in subjective significance. Forebearance, under these circumstances, amounts simply to the existence of such interests or values. This is not simply a matter of
an intellectual choice. Rather, the existence of these general
goals and interests automatically provides a perspective, a set of
dimensions in which a passing whim or an immediate frustration
is experienced. In the absence of such goals and interests, the
immediately present frustration or the promised immediate satisfaction must, accordingly, gain in subjective significance, and,
under these conditions, forebearance or tolerance is unthinka-
ble.[7]

In the absence of such highly developed and stable structures,
then, the impulsive person's prevailing interests—as the patient
with the fallout supply kit idea illustrates—are directed toward
immediate gains and satisfactions. Hence, his interests also tend
to be labile and erratic, shifting according to the mood, personal
requirements, or opportunities of the moment. A context of essentially egocentric and labile interests does not provide a basis
for a high degree of modulation of whim or impulse, nor a basis
for postponement of or resistance to its immediate satisfaction.
On the contrary, where an orientation toward immediate gain
or satisfaction prevails, the given whim or impulse is likely to be
provided only with a well-practiced set of techniques and facili-
ties for quick accomplishment of its aims. This, of course, also
represents an integrative process, but it is a relatively primitive
one as compared with the normal person's.

---

[7] In a recent paper, Jean Piaget gives the same analysis of "will." An act
of "will," he suggests, such as resisting a distraction in order to pursue
work, involves an experience in which the initial appeal of the distraction
is superceded by the greater interest in doing the work and is, therefore,
dependent on pre-existing, long-range goals or values. He summarizes as
follows: "I conclude this exposition: having will is to possess a permanent
scale of values. . . . And conversely, not having will, means knowing only
unstable and momentary values, not being able to rely upon a permanent
scale of values." Jean Piaget, "Will and Action," *Bulletin of the Menninger Clinic*, XXVI, No. 3 (May 1962), 144.

It is well to remember, however, that the impulsive style may, in certain areas of living, be quite adaptive. Those areas seem, in general, to be ones where readiness for quick action or expression and / or a facility and competence of a sort that may be developed in pursuit of immediate and egocentric interests can be useful. It is well known, for example, that many impulsive people possess considerably social facility and are often socially very charming and engaging. They may also be quite playful, in contrast, for instance, to the heavy, overdelibrate, and somewhat dull quality of some obsessive-compulsive people, and, given a good intellectual endowment, they may be witty and entertaining. There is no doubt, also, that many actual as well as fictional "men of action," men with excellent practical competency and a capacity for quick and unhesitating action, are characterized by this general style of functioning. I shall try to show that the mode of cognitive functioning associated with this general style also contributes to these types of competency and facility.

The Impulsive Mode of Cognition

I have referred to the conspicuous lack of long-range planning by impulsive people. It might be imagined that this deficiency is a special and isolated one that simply follows from an inclination to quick action. Actually, however, lack of planning is only one feature of a style of cognition and thinking in which active concentration, capacity for abstraction and generalization, and reflectiveness in general are all impaired. The fact is that the cognition of impulsive people is characterized by an insufficiency of active integrative processes that is comparable to the insufficiency of integrative processes on the affective side.

Let us consider, first, what may simply be called the *judgment* of these people, since it happens to be especially easy to observe. Anyone who does observe an impulsive person's judgment will certainly describe it as poor; it has often been further described by such terms as "arbitrary" or "reckless." The impulsive person, for example, is well known for his capacity to rush into an unlikely business deal or ill-advised marriage. There is a cognitive aspect to this behavior, a judgment, that, as it were, collaborates with the inclination to act. The business deal looks good to him although it would look like a very dim prospect indeed to almost anyone else; this girl—on the shortest of acquaintances— is the one to marry; and even—as in the following illustration— an essentially hopeless criminal act looks as if it can be pulled off.

A forty-year-old man had a history of various kinds of impulsive behavior before entering psychotherapy. For some years, he had gambled heavily; on several occasions, he had abruptly quit what seemed to be a rather good job; and, most recently, he had written several bad checks. After a brief period of contrition, during which he declared with more emphasis than conviction that this sort of thing would surely bring him to a bad end, he described his thinking on the occasion of writing the checks. He had thought at the time that "somehow" he would be able to carry it off without being caught; "probably," he would be able to get the money from such and such a source in time; and, if not, he had "guessed" that he would be able to get it from so and so. True enough, he added, things had not worked out that way at all, and he could see now that it was quite out of the question that they should; nevertheless, at the time that was his thinking. He added only one other comment, to the effect that he supposed that "in a way [he] really knew better."

Vague as it was, his story sounded convincing. It sounded, in other words, as if his thinking *had* been approximately as he described it and as if he *had* vaguely "guessed" that he would be able to carry it off. Yet, one has to agree that, in a certain sense, his last comment, that he "really knew better," is justified. His analysis after the fact shows a clear and reasonable understanding that his chances of success or, in this case, of escape had been small, and it hardly seems likely that this fact or the knowledge on which it is based had come to his attention for the first time after the event in question. He knows all the right answers now, and, undoubtedly, he had known them before. One can only conclude that he had managed to avoid asking himself the questions.

Asking such questions, self-critical, active searching of the first impression or vague hunch, organizing information and considering possibilities—this process is exactly that in which the normal process of judgment consists. It is this process that, in general, is absent in the "judgment" of the impulsive person. It was not pertinent information that was lacking or unavailable to this man but rather the active, searching attention and organizing process that normally puts such information to use. This is, of course, not a black-or-white matter, and, in the case of many impulsive people, as was true also of this patient, a certain self-critical process does occur, but it is a perfunctory and insufficient one. Thus, this man, even before a gambling loss, would go through the motions of a critical evaluation of his chances, perhaps even with the most sober and dutiful expression; meanwhile, his real attention was on the problem of picking the first horse.

The active, searching, critical process that we call judgment, a process that the obsessional person carries out in the manner of a dutiful prayer and at great length and that the normal person carries out relatively smoothly and automatically, is abbreviated or eliminated by the impulsive person. Such a process is not his style. If other factors move him to quick action, the nature of his judgment or, more accurately, his substitute for judgment facilitates such action, allows it to "look good" to him, and allows him to remain oblivious to the drawbacks or complications that would give another person pause and might otherwise give him pause as well.

When we say, therefore, that the impulsive person's judgment is poor, we say something about his cognition in general, namely, that it is deficient in certain active processes. Where the normal person searches, weighs, and develops an initial impression, the impulsive person experiences a more immediate response; his initial impression, hunch, or guess becomes, without much further development, his final conclusion. His thinking is "off the top of the head." I have previously described the hysterical mode of cognition, which is marked by similar deficiencies, as impressionistic; impulsive cognition, where the deficiency of active, searching, critical attention is more severe, may be described as "passive" and "concrete." [8] I will explain what I mean by these terms with the help of another illustration of impulsive "bad judgment."

An impulsive young woman was offered a job in a business operation that was quite shaky and possibly shady as well. The job promised to pay well, and she did need money badly. This fact, the promise of good pay, was, therefore, the first thing that struck her about the offer, and in this her reaction was certainly not different from what others' would be in similar circumstances. However, there were also important unattractive features about the job. It required travel through many small towns without guarantee of comfortable accommodations, reliance on some associates whom she neither cared for nor trusted, and so on.

These serious drawbacks, later confirmed, were apparent from the woman's own initial description of the job. Yet they were not apparent to her, that is, she did not pay attention to them. Instead, she took the job without further ado and then quit it after a few weeks. By this time, the discomforts of traveling were most immediate and most impressive to her, while the fact of her bills and creditors had receded into the background.

I wish to show several things by this illustration. First, if we say that the impulsive person's attention does not search actively and analytically, we may add that his attention is quite easily and completely captured; he sees what strikes him, and what strikes him is not only the starting point of a cognitive

---

[8] The reader should understand that such description always implies the qualification "relatively." No thinking can be completely passive and concrete and certainly not in nonpsychotic people. I am speaking here of a comparative tendency.

integrative process, but also, substantially, it is its conclusion. In this sense, his cognition may be called *passive*.[9] Second, if he does not search—critically examine this aspect and that aspect— he does not perceive things in their potential and logical significance, but sees them only in their most obvious, immediately personally relevant qualities. In this sense, the impulsive mode of cognition is relatively *concrete*. Thus, the woman in the above example does not notice the implied and potential drawbacks of the job offered her, but is captured by its promise of fulfilling her pressing need for money.

The limitations of this general cognitive mode are manifested in various familiar ways, some of which have already been indicated. Planning, concentration, logical objectivity, and reflectiveness in general are all impaired in impulsive people; each of these requires a kind of cognition for which the impulsive character is not equipped. Planning, like judgment, involves shifting attention among various possibilities and directing attention not merely to what is striking or impressive now, but also to what might be important in the future. In general, cognition that is concrete is inevitably dominated by the present, and, in such cognition, the significance of the distant future shrinks. Concentration implies sharply focused, sustained attention and intense examination; it is impaired whenever the characteristic mode of cognition is passively responsive to and, therefore, distracted by the next striking thing that comes along.[10] Reflectiveness, in general, implies turning over a situation in one's mind,

---

[9] The meaning of the term "passive" here is closely similar to the meaning given it by David Rapaport, "Some Metapsychological Considerations Concerning Activity and Passivity" (unpublished MS, 1953). See also David Shapiro, "Color Response and Perceptual Passivity," *Journal of Projective Techniques*, XX, No. 1 (1956), 52–69.

[10] This impairment is very familiar to psychological testers. It is reflected, for instance, in the relatively poor performance of these people on the arithmetic test of the Wechsler-Bellevue Intelligence Scale. It is usually evident also in their general behavior during testing, such as their quick look—rarely sustained examination—at a Rorschach card.

again an active shifting of attention now to this aspect and now to that. Similarly, objectivity—or what is sometimes called the capacity to "take distance"—requires attention that is directed not only to what is immediately interesting, striking, or relevant to the concerns of the observer, but also to what is significant in a more general or more permanent sense. Passive, concrete cognition, therefore, is not objective cognition, but, on the whole, is egocentric.

Here, too, however, I must emphasize that, when I describe these limitations, I am speaking only comparatively. The intelligence of impulsive characters is not a planning, abstracting, reflective intelligence, but neither is it immobilized or disorganized. On the contrary, these people often have keen practical intelligence, intelligence, in other words, that is suited to the competent execution of their short-range, immediate aims. Even exceedingly impulsive people to whom planning or reflectiveness would be altogether alien, in their quick impression or "sizing up" of just those aspects of a situation that are pertinent to their most immediate personal interests, may function with a certain effectiveness. They "operate," and they may be very good at it. Consider the following example.

On an occasion of visiting a prison, I was walking with the prison psychologist through an exercise yard that was occupied by a large crowd of convicts. We were going only a short distance to another building and had been in the yard only a few minutes when a convict approached us, walked directly to my host, and presented a request for a special favor with some considerable charm. It was clear from his manner that he had quickly perceived that the presence of the psychologist in the yard with "company" offered an excellent opportunity to press for the favor. This young man was described to me later as a bright but extremely impulsive and psychopathic person, a repeatedly convicted criminal, and a man who frequently was in trouble inside the prison as well as outside. Here, then, in a man who is probably neither planful, reflective, nor in possession of good judgment, is immediate, highly egocentric thinking that is nevertheless quite effective.

The example, incidentally, raises an interesting question about the commonly held belief that these people are quite incapable of empathy. It would seem, rather, that this man demonstrated an empathic perception that was quite impressive, despite its being of a very limited sort. It is true that, in all likelihood, he felt little interest in and may have been little aware of the psychologist's feelings as such. His awareness and his interest were probably limited essentially to what was immediately relevant to his own current requirements, but it was sensitive awareness nonetheless. Whether one chooses to call this "empathy" is, perhaps, not an important matter. It is, however, a kind of psychological sensitivity that is common to—and, if not understood, it may seem quite paradoxical—many narcissistic-impulsive people who, despite a limited or only exploitative interest in other people, may yet be quite expert and perceptive in the social manipulations that their interests require.

It is interesting to note that cognitive processes do not occupy the same position in the total operation of the impulsive individual, particularly vis-à-vis immediate needs or impulses, as they do in the normal person. Normally, we consider cognitive and thought processes as a whole to be among those factors that promote individual stability. Planning, reflection, judgment, and objectivity tend, in normal functioning, to stabilize against erratic and impulsive action. For example, an impulse to quit a job because it is frustrating on a particular day tends to be restrained by the consideration that it is not frustrating on most days or that it is a necessary step toward a better job. Sometimes, therefore, reflection militates against a given impulse; sometimes, also, it contributes to the development of a whim or impulse into an active and sustained aim or plan. In either case, however, cognition in the normal person tends to collaborate with the stable affective structures I have described against the immediate discharge of an unmodulated whim or impulse.

In the case of the impulsive character, on the other hand,

cognition does not perform such a stabilizing function. Here, awareness is dominated by the immediately striking and personally relevant, that is, by that which is relevant to the need or impulse of the moment. The impulsive person does not search further, he does not "take distance," and his awareness of long-range or logically important considerations is limited. Such a mode of cognition cannot stabilize against speedy action on a whim or impulse; on the contrary, it *serves* the immediate whim or impulse.

One may go further. From the viewpoint that such cognition provides, the world can only be seen as discontinuous and inconstant—a series of opportunities, temptations, frustrations, sensuous experiences, and fragmented impressions. Such cognition and such experience of the world not only fails to stabilize against impulsive action, but even promotes it. Where, for instance, awareness is dominated by the immediate frustration of the job and where there is no sense of logical proportions or future possibilities, there will be no restraint. Indeed, given such a subjective world, restraint would be meaningless, and intelligence could only have the function of arranging the speedy action.

The mode of cognition and the mode of affective functioning fit or mesh in this way, and it is virtually impossible to separate them. It would be possible to argue for the psychological primacy of either of them. One could argue, in other words, that the impulsive person does not search beyond the immediately relevant present because his interests and emotional involvements are limited to immediate gains and satisfactions. But one could equally well argue that the limitations of his cognition and the domination of his awareness by the immediately striking, concrete, and personally relevant interferes with the development of long-range interests or enduring values and aims. Such arguments would, I believe, be specious. Both areas of functioning and the modes that respectively characterize them exist together, each is hardly imaginable without the other, and, in all likelihood, they develop together. The two modes share essential features; immediacy of experience and expression of impulse is paralleled by immediacy of cognitive response. The insufficiency of basic affective structures that are essential equipment for integrative development of a given whim or impulse may well be paralleled by an insufficiency of basic cognitive equipment. For example, a firm sense of objective, independent reality, of permanence, of time, and the like, may be part of the basic cognitive equipment that is deficient in these people. Here, however, we are on ground that must be covered by developmental research.

Before proceeding to the application of this general understanding of impulsive style to two specific varieties of it, I would like to return to a problem that I referred to in the Introduction. It is, in my opinion, a basic problem in understanding and treating impulsive people, and its solution can easily serve, also, to summarize some of the principles of their style.

The problem may be presented in the form of an imaginary question by an impulsive patient.

You see, I can't control myself. I cannot control these impulses. I know that people are right when they say that I will get into trouble, but I can't help it. Surely, you agree that I can't help it. I know that you are a determinist and that you recognize the power of the unconscious. Don't you agree?

How can we answer this question, not only to the patient, but also to ourselves? How can we reconcile our agreement that we are, indeed, determinists and do recognize unconscious forces with our impression that he somehow takes advantage of that fact? The "marionette" viewpoint in psychiatry (see pp. 20 ff.) cannot help us very much; it would force us to simply answer, "Yes." But there is a different answer.

No, I do not agree with the sense of your statement, for when you say that you "cannot" stop, you imply that you want to stop; at least, you imply that that is your predominant conscious wish. I do not believe that is so. Your feelings in the matter are probably quite mixed. You may feel that other people think you should stop, you may even feel yourself that you should stop, you may sometimes feel repentant about not stopping, and, indeed, I expect that, if you thought you were doing this deliberately, you would feel even more uncomfortable about it. But all of that is not the same thing as wanting to stop.

You mention the long-range possibility of getting into trouble, but about this I would say much the same thing. You may feel that you should pay attention to long-range possibilities, be interested in them, and that they should be more important to you than your immediate satisfaction. But I do not think that they *are* that important to you or that you *are* that interested in them.

So, you see, I do not agree with what you mean when you say, "I cannot stop it," since I do not think you are predominantly interested in doing so. But you are quite right about one thing—I am a determinist, and I do not believe that you or anyone else can control at will what you want or do not want or are or are not interested in.[11]

---

[11] This formulation owes much to the therapeutic ideas of Hellmuth Kaiser. See Hellmuth Kaiser, "The Problem of Responsibility in Psychotherapy," *Psychiatry*, 18, No. 3 (1955), 208–209.

Impulsive Styles: Variants

In this chapter, certain features of two special cases or variants of the impulsive style, the psychopathic character and the passive character, are considered briefly. I present these variants not only for their intrinsic interest and importance, but also as samples of the range covered by that style. Each also provides opportunity for discussion of certain issues of more general significance.

Some Psychopathic Traits

In many respects, the psychopath is the very model of the impulsive style. He exhibits in a thorough and pervasive way what for others is only a direction or tendency. He acts on whim, his aim is the quick, concrete gain, and his interests and talents are in ways and means. From a long-range point of view, his behavior is usually erratic, but, from the short-range point of view, it is often quite competent. I will try to show here how certain of his traits—his deficiency of conscience and his proclivity to lying and insincerity—are consistent with the general forms of impulsive functioning and how they may be understood as special features of a special case of this general style.

MORALITY AND CONSCIENCE

The superego has been understood in psychoanalysis as arising from the impact on the child (in a given instinctual state) of external authority and prohibition, the result of this process being an internalization (introjection) of that authority and prohibition. Two sources, therefore, are held accountable, in somewhat different weights, for the specific, individual form of the superego or pathological superego formations: first, in some measure, the specific, individual quality and intensity of the child's instinctual state and, second and mainly, the nature of the material available for this internalization. For example, superego pathology is commonly attributed to the absence, inconsistency, or excessive harshness of parental authority.

To these two general determinants of the quality of the superego, however, it seems reasonable to add a third: the status of various ego functions—specifically, the nature of the existing mode of thinking, the prevailing forms of emotional experience, and the like—that are likely to be involved in this transformation of external authority into internal attitudes, experience, and affects. However this developmental question of the original determinants of the superego may be answered, it seems beyond doubt that the ultimate adult form of the superego or, perhaps I should say, the form of those superego components and manifestations that are present in the individual's conscious subjective experience—conscience, moral values, and the like—cannot be independent of the modes of thought and subjective experience that characterize him generally.

The following question arises: What general modes of thought and subjective experience are prerequisites for normal moral values and conscience? To this, we can add another question: Are normal moral values and conscience imaginable in the context of the impulsive modes of functioning I have described? I will attempt to answer these questions, although the answers will necessarily be brief and incomplete.

For this purpose, it is best to separate the problem of moral values from the problem of conscience. First, let us consider the nature of moral values—moral values considered as interests or aims. Such moral values as justice, truth, or personal integrity are, in the first place, exceedingly abstract interests or aims. They are ideals. Their goal is the fulfillment of abstract principles, their satisfaction is intangible and often incomplete, and their viewpoint is, at the least, long range. These values are also, in a certain sense, impersonal, that is, they are more or less objectively defined and are relatively independent of and removed from immediate personal preferences or interests. For example, the just course of action for an individual may coincide with his own immediate advantage or may run counter to it; even in the latter case, however, if justice is an important value, it may well outweigh the immediate advantage in subjective emotional significance. It is clear, also, that moral values or ideals, if they are subjectively important at all, are relatively stable and continuous. These values, in other words, and, perhaps, ideals generally must be considered as highly developed and refined aims or interests; they stand in contrast to interest in concrete, immediate gains or satisfactions not only in their content, but also in their form.

The existence of moral values requires, therefore, a certain level of affective development, a capacity, in general, for emotional involvement in interests of an intangible sort and relatively remote from immediate personal needs. It is likely, also, that their existence requires a certain cognitive development— a long-range, general viewpoint and a degree of reflectiveness seem to be part of any appreciation of or respect for principles. It is not surprising, then, that such moral values as justice develop only slowly and over a long period of time in normal children.[1] And it is hardly imaginable that such values or ideals

---

[1] See Jean Piaget, *The Moral Judgment of Children* (Glencoe, Ill.: Free Press, n.d.).

could develop to any great degree in the context of a general style in which interests are limited to immediate, concrete gains or satisfactions and in which awareness is dominated by the personally relevant present.

It may be argued that having moral values is not necessarily just a matter of respect for abstract principles or ideals, but also involves more personal interests and, in a sense, more practical justifications. Thus, the humanitarian may argue that his interest in social justice is not only a matter of principle, but also a matter of broad human sympathies; the sociologist may point out that respect for law and principles of social regulation is a social necessity and potential protection and advantage for each individual; the scientist might say that he values truth because science is impossible without it; and the artist might say that he has high standards for no loftier or more moral reason than a devotion to art.

It is true that abstract moral values, respect for principles and ideals, usually exist in a context of other, quasimoral values and interests of a social, ideological, intellectual, or even aesthetic sort. But all these values, aims, or interests are quite abstract, all are long range and relatively far removed from immediate, concrete gain or advantage to the individual. Indeed, all of them may easily run counter to some immediate gain. In other words, all are quite highly developed, stable, and continuous aims or interests, and these interests, too, would seem to require a relatively highly developed affective organization as well as cognition that comfortably and habitually extends beyond the immediately relevant present. These quasimoral values and interests, which are only indistinctly separable from moral ideals, are therefore equally unlikely to appear in the thoroughgoing impulsive character. He does not have the affective or cognitive equipment for them.

The experience and functioning of conscience is by no means simply equivalent to the possession of or respect for moral values. Conscience involves a distinctive experience—an experience of "I should" or "I ought." (See Chap. 2.) The "should" or "ought" of conscience always implies a reference to a moral standard—"I should" (according to . . .)—sometimes, in the form of a general moral principle but, sometimes, merely in the form of a concrete authority, a respected person. The experience involves, then, a view of one's self or one's actions, frequently a disapproving view, from the standpoint of some principle or authority. This quasi-external view of oneself is what we mean by the "inner watchman" or "inner voice" of conscience.

The experience of conscience, therefore, is dependent on the capacity of the individual for a certain detachment from himself, on self-critical attention and examination. Self-critical examination of a piece of behavior—in the case of the obsessive-compulsive, examination of virtually every piece of behavior—from the standpoint of a moral standard, may sometimes involve quite abstract dimensions and considerations. A piece of behavior, meaning also a thought or a motive, may be examined for its implicit or potential moral significance, for what it "means" morally, for what the consequences would be if everyone did it, and the like, quite aside from its practical significance.

For instance, a patient decided that to visit a prostitute is wrong because the action implicitly gives assent to and supports the institution of prostitution with all its attendant evils and injustices; he hardly considered the actual consequences of the specific act.

Even in the case, however, in which the self-critical examination is from a more concrete standpoint—for example, what would my father (teacher, . . .) think about this—detached attention is required, attention that focuses back on the individual's own thoughts or behavior, judging this aspect or that aspect from a special standpoint.

Detached and self-critical attention such as this is, among all neurotic styles, probably most characteristic of the obsessive-compulsive; such a form of thinking is manifest in his conscience, in his doubting, and in that outstanding obsessional symptom that seems to stand somewhere between doubting and conscience—worrying. But this form of thinking is quite alien to the impulsive style. I do not mean that impulsive characters never experience pangs of conscience, but only that the more thoroughly the individual is characterized by this style, the more perfunctory and limited his conscience will be.

Egocentrically unself-critical cognitive orientation and passive immediacy and concreteness of cognition are not consistent with such a self-critical examination. Indeed, I have tried to show that the general limitations in this style of thinking of self-critical appraisal and detached, actively searching attention are such as to impair even common judgment and logical objectivity in these people. It does not seem to be stretching the similarity of form to speak of a self-critical "inner voice" of judgment as well as of conscience and to say that the latter is not likely to be much developed if even the thought requirements of the former are lacking. Similarly, one may ask if a way of thinking that neglects even that which is logically of potential or implicit significance in favor of the immediately impressive or personally relevant is likely to be concerned with potential or implicit moral significance. Altogether, in other words, an individual who does not generally reconsider an initially tempting action because of what its logical consequences may mean to him two months from now is surely unlikely to reconsider this action in terms of its abstract moral significance, its moral "meaning," what such behavior might mean to the general social order if everybody did it, or the like.

One final point may be added here. If it is true that the individual characterized in extreme by this style is neither accustomed to nor equipped for the general self-critical thought that is one of the essential bases for conscience, it is also true that these people are lacking in another sort of basis, equally essential, in the general nature of their mode of action and their subjective experience of action. I refer here to the impairment in these people of a subjective sense of deliberateness and intention and to the general attenuation of phases preparatory to action. It is not only that these preparatory phases—planning, anticipation, and the like—constitute perhaps the most critical occasion (although not the only one) when conscience would normally operate, but also that a sense of moral responsibility seems to require a sense of actual responsibility, that is, intentionality, deliberateness, and choice among alternatives. If an individual characteristically acts too immediately to feel the weight of himself wanting, considering, deciding, and then doing, not only does a critical time for the operation of conscience disappear, but also a significant part of its subject matter disappears.

Thus, a remarkable attitude is observable in psychopathic people when they regard an action that, in someone else, would produce pangs of conscience, it is a those-are-the-fortunes-of-war attitude, an attitude that says, "Too bad, but it's nobody's fault —anyone would have done the same thing in those circumstances." This attitude is remarkable not only for its absence of conscience, but also for its absence of a sense of having chosen to act in this particular way—having acted deliberately when there were alternative possibilities.

For example, a criminal who had held up a bar was asked by a television interviewer why he had brutally pistol-whipped a patron who had been standing near him. He answered, with a little shrug, that this (unarmed) patron had started to move toward him, and his answer seemed to imply that his reaction was simply a reflexive one that anyone would share. He seemed convincingly oblivious to the innumerable alternative possibilities—retreating, threatening, and the like—that were objectively available.

Thus, conscience and moral values are not elemental psychological faculties, but involve and depend on a number of cognitive and affective functions. Morality, therefore, will "take," flourish, and, in turn, influence and possibly contribute to various more general aspects of the over-all style in certain contexts, whereas in others it will not. In the impulsive style generally, including the range of diagnostic categories I indicated at the beginning of the previous chapter, moral values are likely to be comparatively underdeveloped and uninfluential, and conscience is likely to be perfunctory. But this trait is especially pronounced and has, incorrectly but commonly, even become the major defining feature of that affectively and cognitively more primitive variant of this general style that we diagnose as psychopathic character. The psychopath does not necessarily reject morality, and he certainly does not reject conventional morality, as others may do, on principle, that is, in favor of different and possibly more independently conceived values. It is more accurate to say that he is simply uninterested in morality. That is, he is uninterested in a system of moral values or principles as something to be believed in, although he may be perfectly well aware of social morality as a fact to be dealt with, for example, to be deferred to when it is practical to do so. From a moral standpoint, therefore, he is cynical; but, from his own concrete and practical standpoint, he is merely possessed of good sense.[2]

PSYCHOPATHIC INSINCERITY AND LYING

Insincerity and lying are common traits in psychopathic characters, and it is obvious that they have some relationship to a deficiency of moral values and conscience. There are two possibilities for such a relationship. First, these traits may simply follow from a lack of conscience, lack of a feeling of responsibility to be truthful or genuine; I believe this would be the most gen-

---

[2] I know that some psychiatrists and psychologists, particularly those without much institutional experience, will deny that major differences in conscience or morality, other than differences in content, really exist and will even deny the existence of "old-fashioned psychopaths." I do not believe in pure types, in the case of this or any other style; but I think that these people overlook plain facts, perhaps partly because of exclusive concern with psychological dynamics and mental contents.

erally accepted understanding. There is a second possibility, however, that seems to me more likely, namely, that the lack of conscience and morality, on the one hand, and the insincerity and lying, on the other, are essentially and independently related to the same general psychopathic modes of functioning. An interesting finding of psychological testers seems to support this view. Psychologists have found that the tendency to fabricate, as the psychopath does, can be inferred from projective tests, although those tests require only imaginative and not factual responses. There is, in other words, no obligation to "tell the truth" on these tests, no possibility of actual lying, and no issue of conscience of that sort involved; yet, it is possible to identify certain forms of thinking that are characteristic of people given to lying and insincerity. The question then arises: What special forms of thinking do characterize psychopathic fabrication?

The fact that psychopathic people are capable of lying or insincerity in no way distinguishes them from anyone else. Even the fact that they are more often insincere than others distinguishes them only roughly, since it is easy to imagine any person in circumstances where continued lying and insincerity would be warranted and likely. But what is certainly distinctive about the psychopath is that he lies so easily and so fluently. As we sometimes say, he is "glib."

When we call an idea or an expression "glib," we are actually describing a special and, in some respects, extreme form of the impulsive style of thinking and behavior. We mean that the idea is not a product of reflection or deliberation, but is an impression or passing thought that is expressed without critical examination. It is "off the top of the head." The psychopath responds to a factual question or to a Rorschach inkblot as it strikes him or as whim or circumstances move him at the moment.

It is for this reason that one may easily have the feeling that what he says, when he flips back an answer to a question, does not represent what he "really" thinks or that he "really" means what he says, whether or not the particular answer is actually the truth. And, sure enough, he does not hesitate to say something quite different five minutes later. He does not have the attitude of objectivity, the deliberateness, or the interest in logical cohesiveness that characterizes the normal individual even when engaged in imaginative production, that is, even when deliberately putting aside ordinary standards of factual truth. These are not primarily matters of moral scruple on the part of the normal person or the lack of them on the part of the psychopathic character; they are matters of interest and automatic cognitive tendency. The glibness and unself-critical immediacy of the psychopath's ideas and thinking are not, in themselves, lying or insincerity, but they narrow and blur the subjective distance, so to speak, between sincerity and insincerity, and they comprise one essential basis for the fluent insincerity that is characteristic of him. Glibness is one of the critical features from which psychologists may be able to infer a proclivity toward lying from a projective test.

But if the psychopath's glibness enables us to understand something of the fluency and ease of his insincerity, it still does not explain its aim from his standpoint.

For example, a psychopathic patient enters a psychologist's office, where he is scheduled to take a Rorschach test. He makes a point of his friendly interest in the procedure and his eagerness to take the test and states, in fact, that he has had considerable interest in the Rorschach test for some time. His behavior is patently insincere, and his statement of interest is very likely untrue, but what is the actual interest that moves him to insincerity?

In a general way, this question could be answered simply. Very likely, his aim is to get by, to impress the psychologist favorably, to disarm him, or some other interest of approximately this sort. But motivations such as these are certainly not limited to psychopaths; indeed, in the circumstances, such an aim is probably quite common to one extent or another. What, then, distinguishes the psychopath's viewpoint and aims in this situation? The answer is suggested by another feature of his cognition, another variant actually of a general feature of the impulsive style.

The interests and attention of the impulsive character, in general, tend to be dominated by what is of immediate, concrete, personal relevance. In the psychopath, this limitation of interest takes a particular and extreme form. He is forever "operating," he is after some immediate practical gain or advantage, and his attention is on those aspects of his present circumstances that are relevant to such possibilities. He is immersed in the opportunities or exigencies of his circumstances, and such issues as "getting by," winning the other's favor, or disarming or impressing him are not peripheral or sporadic concerns, but central and dominating ones. This fact cannot help but significantly influence a great many of the psychopath's communications.

In normal communication, a certain detached and objective interest in the content of the communication, as opposed to concern with its concrete circumstances, is taken for granted. It is taken for granted, for example, that an ordinary factual question such as, "Where did you go to school?" which may be asked in a variety of circumstances, will be answered in essentially the same way in all of them, assuming that none of these circumstances is truly extraordinary. It is true that we do not expect perfection in this matter, and we are not surprised, for instance, if a neurotic person is interested also, without being clearly aware of this interest, in using the ostensible communication to impress or move his audience in one way or another.[3] Nevertheless, we usually expect that a certain level of detached interest in the content of a communication will be maintained;

---

[3] Hellmuth Kaiser has, in fact, advanced the view that such a distortion of the communication process is a symptom of all neurosis. See Louis B. Fierman, ed., *Effective Psychotherapy: The Contribution of Hellmuth Kaiser* (New York: The Free Press of Glencoe, 1965).

in fact, such detachment or objectivity is so much a part of normal communication that it is not always easy to appreciate its significance or the radical ways in which communication is altered in its absence.

In the case of the psychopath, egocentric interest in the immediate, concrete circumstances of communication often overrides, in his awareness, any detached interest in its objective content. He is, in other words, not so much interested in *what* is said to him as in the possibilities the situation offers. He is, and consciously so, not so much interested in what he says as in how well it works. Again, this is not primarily a matter of moral scruple, but of the limitations and direction of interest and attention.

Both of these related tendencies—unself-critical glibness, on the one hand, and the domination of interest and awareness by concrete, personally relevant circumstances of communication, on the other—seem to work together to produce the fluent insincerity of the psychopath. Perhaps, the question could be raised as to whether, given such a general style of functioning, moral scruples might not still intercede if they were present. The answer would seem to be, however, that it is precisely in such a style of functioning that moral scruples cannot be present to any great degree; the question, therefore, is not a meaningful one. It seems likely that a good deal if not all of the "antisocial" behavior of psychopaths may thus be understood not as the direct or simple consequence of a deficiency of moral values or conscience, but as following rather, together with that deficiency, from extreme and special forms of various features of the impulsive style—egocentric, concrete viewpoint; general lack of aims and values much beyond immediate, tangible gain; and quick, nondeliberate modes of action.

The Passive, "Weak" Character

I have already stated some of the reasons for considering extremely passive characters to be variants of the impulsive style,
and I would like now to add some further explanation of that
view. The explanation is necessary since, from a descriptive
standpoint, the bracketing of these passive people, usually characterized by their apparent inactivity, with more typically action-
oriented impulsive characters may well seem strange. In actual
fact, however, even from a purely descriptive standpoint, the
two groups are not as sharply distinguished as it might seem,
and there are many individuals, for example, many alcoholics,
who could equally well be described as either "passive" or "impulsive."

The essential congruence of the two groups is suggested in a
general way by what is conspicuously absent in both of them,
namely planned, sustained activity associated with a sense of deliberateness. More specifically, there is, first of all, a close similarity in the subjective experience of action and motivation, a
similarity that tends to be obscured by the usual descriptive
terminology. The characteristic passive experiences of being
"weak"—that is, unable to resist temptation—being pushed or
seduced into action, or "giving in" are experiences that contain
the same impairment and attenuation of the normal sense of
deliberateness and intention, and contain the same sense of partial or exceedingly transient motivation that characterizes the
impulsive person in general. This attenuation of the feeling of
deliberateness forms the nucleus, in the passive character just as
in the impulsive character, of the defensive disavowal of responsibility, particularly in the form of so-called externalization of
responsibility. Furthermore, this attenuation of experience is associated in the passive character, as it is in the impulsive character, with an attenuation or "short-circuiting" of integrative processes.

Among passive characters, there are those in whom what may be described as passive-impulsiveness—that is, "giving in" to temptation—seems to be somewhat the more prominent mode, and there are others in whom passive-submissiveness—that is, "giving in" to pressure—seems predominant. The first mode is more obviously related to the general impulsive style, whereas the second, the passive-submissive, is a somewhat more special variant of that style and warrants further discussion. Among truly impulsive and passive characters, passive-submissive people seem to lead the least unplanned lives. They do not dart erratically, and they do not drift altogether aimlessly; they drift, but the direction of that drift, as it were, seems to be a compromise between the prevailing current and a degree of planned steering. These people locate external pressures that appear to gain weight in their subjective experience exactly because of the relative deficiency of autonomous direction. These pressures seem to fulfill certain of the psychological functions normally fulfilled by internal executive apparatuses.

One such patient was a thirty-five-year-old male homosexual. This man was competent in a theatrical profession, but he had followed it only off and on and certainly had no real career. He maintained that the course of his life—where he had lived, whom he had been associated with, the sort of work that he did—had not really been chosen by him but had been determined by various fortuitous pressures and circumstances. He felt, in other words, that his history was one of having "given in" repeatedly. Thus, he had originally been seduced into homosexual activity and then had been subjected to pressure from successive partners to continue homosexual life. Such and such a person had "insisted" that he move here or there or do this or that. Actually, he led a quiet life and, aside from his homosexuality, almost a conventional one, but this way of life, too, he maintained, followed from his concerns with what various people—his neighbors, his boss, and others— might expect of him rather than from any preference of his own.

Altogether, he made a good case for his contention that his life had been directed by external circumstances and pressures; in every instance, he was able to identify the pressure or the person responsible for his action. It was only that none of these pressures seemed objectively very compelling, together with the fact that his life actually had had a certain continuity, that reminded one that he had made choices along the way and showed that he was not devoid of plan.

This patient, in other words, exaggerates the extent to which his life actually has been determined by force of accidental, external circumstances; the circumstances bear too many marks of consistent selection. On the other hand, there is little doubt that external pressures did make some unusual contribution to the course of his life and that he did "give in" to these pressures on many occasions. The extent to which his life is relatively aimless and lacking in active plans, goals, or development bears witness to this. How can we understand this process?

Active planning is not an all-or-none matter. Passive-submissive people seem to plan, but they plan only vaguely.[4] Similarly, they may have relatively sustained intentions, goals, and interests—more so than the typical impulsive character does —but these, also, are likly to be vague and indefinite. Given this state, an impressive temptation or a forceful pressure will evoke not a normally detached or normally interested response, but an essentially abrupt action, an immediate response in which any further integrative processes are "short-circuited."

Often passive-submissive people are, implicitly, in an attitude of waiting for a circumstance—a pressure or temptation (or, as was frequent in this patient's case, a seduction, which combines elements of both pressure and temptation)—that will precipitate an action out of a vague intention. Sometimes, waiting is even explicit and quite specific, as in the case of one patient who said, quite convincingly, that he didn't really know if he felt at the time like gambling, but he "sorta felt like going" [5] to a place

---

[4] It may be added, from a dynamic standpoint, that they shrink noticeably from sharper, more well-defined plans.

[5] These people often "sorta feel" like doing something, "kinda think" they will, feel "hungryish," and the like. Such expressions are not mere

where it was quite possible that he would be urged to join a game, adding that he could "always make that decision when the time comes." But it is by no means only a pressure or temptation that, so to speak, meets a vague intention head on and crystallizes it that precipitates action in passive-submissive people. Even a pressure that is quite far removed from the passive person's state of vague intentions or, at least, meets those intentions only very obliquely is nevertheless quite compelling, because of the relative absence of well-defined intentions and aims and a sufficiently critical and detached attitude. These people are, as it were, easily brain-washed.

Let me discuss certain features of this process further, illustrating with a specific instance of "giving in" on the part of the homosexual patient described above.

The patient attended a party with a vague anticipation that he might meet some new sexual partner. As it turned out, however, he was approached by a man of a physical type he does not find "especially" attractive. Nevertheless, when this man pressed his attentions, the patient, as he says, "gave in." As he explained his action, he thought, finally, "Why not? Anyway, he really wasn't *bad* looking. And he [the other man] did want to very much."

One may, of course, comply with another person's request, a friend's, for example, because one likes him and is interested in his welfare or happiness. Such compliance does not objectively look and does not subjectively feel like "giving in." Compliance of this sort, like compliance that arises simply from genuine agreement with another person's point of view, involves active judgment, attention to the pressure or request and whatever recommends it, clear awareness of alternatives, and, finally, a choice, a fully intentional and deliberate act. This patient's compliance, however, was quite different. Certainly, he had not

---

verbal mannerisms or verbal defensive operations, but reflect an actual lack and avoidance of sharpness of experience of motivation or feeling.

come to a genuine agreement with the other's interest; he indicates this clearly by his final emphasis, "And *he* did want to very much." Neither can his action be attributed to attention to and interest in the other person's needs. It is, in fact, highly unlikely that he had any appreciable interest in this man's welfare or happiness. His compliance and the compliance of such people in general is based not on empathic perception of the other person's needs or interest in their pleasure, but on a concrete sensation of the force with which those needs are presented and an interest in immediate relief. To the empathic person interested in satisfying a friend, the superficial matter of whether that friend expresses his request timidly or loudly is unimportant (except as an indicator of underlying need), but this is exactly what is of decisive importance to the passive person. Thus, when the patient says, "He did want to very much," his actual meaning is closer to, "He insisted on it very forcefully."

When a passive person explains an action by saying, "But he expected me to do it," one may easily answer, "And you evidently felt obliged to comply with that expectation of his." Such a reply often evokes surprised recognition in the passive person of a new dimension. The objective fact of his having had a *choice* among possible alternatives is brought to his attention. He had not regarded the external pressure of the other's expectations with that sort of detachment, and he had not considered it or evaluated it; he had simply felt its weight.

The result of such a process is not a judgment of alternatives and a choice made from among them, but a judgment that is aborted by the dimming of alternative possibilities; it is not a completion of integrative processes with a relatively smooth action, but a psychologically premature crystallization of vague intentions into an essentially abrupt and discontinuous action; it is not a subjective feeling of deliberateness and "wanting to," but a feeling of partial, incomplete, and half-hearted motivation. In short, this may be called at least a partially impulsive mode of action.

It may be added that the passive person's report of the experience of "giving in," like the impulsive person's experience of "irresistible impulse," should not be considered simply as an objective report of his inability to help himself despite his wishes. He is not, at that critical point, merely unable to help himself; he is unable to *want* to help himself. The experience of "giving in," therefore, does not express his feeling of being unwillingly overwhelmed by a superior force, but rather his loss of interest at that moment in resisting it.

It is interesting to note that, as my example may already have suggested, male homosexuals are frequently characterized by this passive or passive-impulsive style of functioning and the cognitive, affective, and action modes that comprise it. Thus, these men often lead lives of the sort I have described—relatively unplanned and drifting, although not completely erratic. Especially interesting, however, is the fact that this general style of functioning may help us to understand certain features of the form of their sexuality.

The deviation of the homosexual's sexuality is by no means limited to choice of object or predominant erogenous zone, although these and other contents of sexual deviation have tended to preoccupy psychiatric discussion. These men are also often characterized by marked hypersensuality and, in a certain sense, hypersexuality, as compared with the normal. Frequently, their lives are thoroughly dominated by sexual-sensual activity—sexual activity of great frequency and essentially based on whim, sexuality in which there is relatively little modulation of purely sensuous interest and experience with affective interest and experience and in which even sensuous interest seems quite diffuse, sexuality that is essentially egocentric and that includes little or no further involvement with the partner. This sensuality is not, in my opinion, to be explained by sociological considerations, nor can it be satisfactorily explained by supplementary assumptions of additional fixations involving specific contents.[6] This seems, rather, to be a kind of sexual activity and impulse experience that is simply consistent with the general forms of functioning of this style.

I am suggesting, in other words, that modes of affect, action, and subjective experience that are generally characteristic of an individual are operative in his sexual life as well. Here we approach more general questions that are of considerable interest. I have in mind the general problem of the relationship between instinctual orientation or the content of instincts, on the one hand, and style of functioning, on the other, as well as the more specific problem of the relationship of sex (male or female) to the shape (or "choice") of neurosis.

---

[6] For example, specific fixation on cutaneous sensation is sometimes suggested for such cases. See Otto Fenichel, *The Psychoanalytic Theory of Neurosis* (New York: Norton, 1945), p. 374.

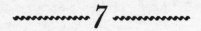

General and Theoretical Considerations

I would like to present here a more general view of styles as I conceive them to be and to consider certain problems of styles from the standpoint of that conception. I would not say that this general view is necessarily essential to the clinical studies. It simply represents the way in which, in the course of the clinical studies, I have imagined styles to function and develop and the way in which I have tried to answer certain general questions about them, some of them troublesome.

I shall consider, first, questions concerning the origin and development of styles. What are their beginnings? How do they rely on innate psychological equipment? How is their development influenced by instinctual drives? Then, continuing the general question of the relationship of styles to drives, what is their significance for drive-tension control and regulation? Finally, what is the relationship of style to defense?

The Initial Organizing Configuration

How can we imagine the beginnings.of relatively stable psychological styles? Are we entitled to say that some kind of elementary style exists from the start, in the newborn baby? If so, what determines its quality? It is safe to say that the capacity, the psychological equipment, for such general functions as we have considered—cognition, affective experience, and the like— is, at least in a rudimentary way, provided for in the human constitution. The elements of this equipment—sensory and perceptual apparatus, memory apparatus, some kind of affect or at least affect-like tension-discharge equipment, and the like— seem to be operative from birth. It is apparent, also, that individual variations in innate equipment are bound to influence the quality of the more developed functions in which it later participates, so they may be regarded as independent sources of individual styles. This much is reasonably evident.

But how, exactly, shall we define the relationship between innate psychological equipment and the beginnings of psychological style? It is still a long and by no means self-evidently direct step, logically speaking, from a picture of an assemblage of innate, certainly rudimentary psychological equipment in the setting, as it seems, of an infant still more or less immediately at the mercy of internal tensions to a picture of generalized, relatively stable, and characteristic modes of functioning or what one could call style. Let me attempt to show, however, that the elements of this picture can be composed in a slightly different way, one that makes the relationship between innate equipment and mode of function clearer and one that suggests that such equipment actually provides a more substantial base for the development of individual style than it appears to do.

It should not be imagined, in the first place, that innate psychological equipment consists of an assemblage of a mere few items—tension and sensory thresholds, cognitive apparatus, and such. We may not yet be able to compile an adequate catalogue of that equipment, but this need not prevent us from recognizing its domain and its significance. The fact is that, leaving instinctual drives aside for the moment, such equipment can be regarded as comprising all, on the psychological side, that constitutes humanness in the newborn baby.

It is not justified, either, to regard the various items of this equipment as isolated and without interrelationships and over-all integration. For instance, the infant's readiness for sucking activity, his readiness to respond to a certain sort of object, and the rapid development, with nursing, of anticipations with regard to that object give evidence of an organized interrelationship of memory, perceptual apparatus, activity patterns, and so forth. In other words, we are at least entitled to regard this equipment as comprising an innate configuration of some considerable complexity. Indeed, the fact is that, far from a picture of a few items of psychological apparatus scattered, as it were, against a background of drive tension, it is difficult to imagine that any biological tension could become psychologically manifest except as it is mediated by one or another aspect of this configuration, however primitive and unspecific that mediation may initially be. I am suggesting, in other words, that a configuration of innate psychological equipment imposes some form and organization, however little differentiated it may be initially, on drives and external stimuli and, in general, on all psychological tensions. More exactly, I mean that such innate apparatus imposes some form and organization on the *subjective experience* of internal tensions and external stimuli from the beginning.

Thus, the experience of hunger, of the impetus to suck, of temperature, light, nipple, or smile all reflect biological tensions or external stimuli that have been mediated by and given a form in subjective experience according to the psychological equipment with which the infant is endowed, the equipment of external and bodily sensation, tension and sensory threshold apparatus, and the like. Individual variations in such equipment imply variations in the experience of tensions and stimuli. Further differences, such as differences in anticipation capacity and the perceptual equipment necessary for object recognition, also soon become involved in the process of subjective tension organization, tending, in one case, to cause drive tensions to be experienced in a more directed form and, in another case, in a more diffuse form. And so on.

To the extent that there are innate organizing and form-giving configurations of psychological apparatus—I suggest the term "initial organizing configuration" for the totality of such equipment—we are obliged to alter our picture of the infant as helpless vis-à-vis his own instinctual drives. To the extent that he is equipped with tension-organizing capacities, he is not, as it were, purely a passive agent and his behavior is not immediately and totally dependent on biological drives or external stimuli. In a manner of speaking, to that extent, he may be said to exist psychologically and his psychology to constitute an autonomous factor in the determination of his behavior. It appears to me that, to that extent, also, one can properly speak of the beginnings of psychological style, of psychological functioning that is a product not of drives and stimuli alone, but also of the mental organizing processes of an individual.

The modification, development, and differentiation of the "initial organizing configuration," of course, proceeds immediately under the influence of the external world it encounters as well as continued maturation. The existence of such a configuration has certain general implications for the future development of the individual as well as his present functioning. If there is such an organization of internal tensions and external stimulation from the beginning, then it follows that all succeeding developmental influences, including both those that originate externally and those that arise internally, are initially organized according to the forms of functioning, the forms of subjective experience, cognition, and the like, that prevail at the time. Development, in other words, always proceeds *through* the existing forms, and these forms, themselves, always develop, as it were, from the inside out, always through transformations and never additively.

The development of *general* forms of functioning is, perhaps, more readily understandable in this light, since it implies that each new developmental influence, as it is incorporated, is stamped by the existing organization. This viewpoint also makes clear that certain developmental influences "take" in a given style, whereas others, no matter how forceful or compelling they may seem from an objective standpoint, do not "take," that is, are inconsistent with or lack foundation in the existing forms of functioning. Without such a general view—as, for example, in the conception that change or development may occur simply by the impression of forceful external circumstances or the incorporation of whole segments of external reality—it would be difficult to understand the very existence of styles or formal consistency in functioning.

Before leaving the subject of innate psychological equipment, I would like to add a few words concerning a related matter, namely, the degree of innate determination of *adult* styles. Let me make the point clear. The considerable significance of innate psychological equipment for the origins of psychological style in infants by no means necessarily implies equivalent or even comparable significance of innate factors for the fully developed and highly differentiated adult style. On the contrary, innate factors of the sort we have in mind can only be responsible for form tendencies of a very general and not a highly differentiated or specific kind. In general, the more specific the style feature, the less the innate responsibility for it. On the other hand, however, that much—innate determination of exceedingly general style tendencies—seems quite likely.

An interesting example of this, although certainly not one without ambiguities, is the existence of certain differences in the affinities of the sexes for different neurotic conditions. There seems to be an overwhelming predominance of women among hysterical patients, whereas there is a relative predominance of men among obsessive-compulsives. Relationships such as these between biological sex and the shape of neurosis cannot be easily understood from the standpoint of dynamic or symptom content alone or even from the standpoint of the specific defense mechanisms respectively characteristic of the neurotic conditions. But, from the formal standpoint, the existence not of specific innate determinants of the neurosis, certainly, but of innate sex differences in general style tendencies that are reflected in the shape of neurosis, should neurosis develop, is readily understandable and perhaps even obvious. I have in mind such sex differences in style tendencies as the general mode of activity, perhaps certain features of cognitive attitude, and the like.

Instinctual Drives and Style Development

There can hardly be any question about whether instinctual drives influence the development of psychological style, but only in what ways and in what measure. The unfolding of new drives with new urges and motivations, new potentialities of subjective experience, objects of interest, kinds of activity, and modes of activity[1] certainly have an impact on the existing fabric or configuration of mental organizing forms. But what is the outcome of this impact?

The simplest and most apparent possibility is that each phase of instinctual drive development freshly stamps and reshapes all forms of mental functioning according to its own mode. But this conception fails for several reasons. In the first place, there simply is no evidence that cognitive modes, general forms of subjective experience, and the like, are in fact subject to such radical upheavals. On the contrary, all that we can see points in the opposite direction, to their relative stability and slowness to change. Second and more specifically, however, such a conception does not take into account the general implications of the prior existence of an organizing configuration for *any* new developmental force. Whereas qualities inherent in the particular

---

[1] "Modes of activity" is used here in Erikson's sense. Erik H. Erikson, *Childhood and Society* (New York: Norton, 1950).

drive tension tend to exercise a modifying force on, for example, the general mode of affective experience, those modes will also have had a prior influence on the affective quality of the drive tension. It is comparable, to a certain degree, with the fact that people learn mostly according to their preconceptions; this is not to say that those preconceptions are unalterable, but it certainly does imply a conservative human tendency in the face of a new set of facts. At any rate, the impact of a fresh drive tension on an existing configuration of organizing forms is certainly not a simple matter, but involves a rather complex interplay between the two.

Let us start by imagining more clearly one side of this interplay, the nature of the modifying force—the impact that, other things aside for the moment, an emerging drive tension tends to exert on a given configuration or fabric of organizing forms. That impact resides essentially in the fact that the emergence of any given drive tension confronts the existing forms with all the potentialities for fresh kinds of function and new qualities of experience intrinsic to *it*. These potentialities are very great and are by no means limited to the experience and function of the drive itself. A drive tension and its mode are only the focal point of the unfolding of a whole broad front of new developments, including the maturation of new physical and muscular capacities and new behavioral tendencies.[2]

Insofar as the drive provides impetus to fresh kinds of activity and interests, it engages not only physical and muscular capacities, but cognitive ones as well, in new ways. It moves its subject into new relationships not only with the physical world, but also with the human and social world and here engages affective capacities. In other words, such a development has potentialities for rapid and remarkably extensive emergence of new psychological functions and kinds of subjective experience. As it looks so far, these potentialities would seem to be for the most profound

_____

2 See Erik H. Erikson, *loc. cit.*

and radical effects on the existing organizing forms. But they are only potentialities. Let us imagine now the ways in which such potentialities may (or may not) be realized.

A drive tension cannot spring into being fully developed and sharply articulated. On the contrary, it must initially be exceedingly diffuse subjectively, an impetus, let us say, toward certain external objects and actions. This diffuse impetus is enough, however, to move its subject into the external world, to move it toward actions and toward objects or, at least in the case of the baby, toward behavior that normally causes the object to come to it. In the course of this actual experience and depending on the nature of the external object and circumstances, the initially diffuse tension becomes organized into new qualities of subjective experience, new qualities of affect and satisfaction, and new kinds of behavior.

For example, the baby cries initially not for its mother, nor with an expectation of satisfaction, nor even with a sense of its need, but only, we may imagine, from discomfort. The mother responds, and the baby is satisfied. In the course of such experience, the initially diffuse tension becomes organized into a more directed tension, into an experience of need eventually directed clearly toward the mother.[3] Along with this directedness, anticipations of satisfaction appear, perhaps a sense of expectancy and trust, and, with these, a greater capacity to endure delays in satisfaction.

Thus, many new qualities of subjective experience come into being. Anticipation capacity is advanced, an affective experience begins, and a new drive-tension organization form is created, all determined, first, by the potentialities inherent in the drive and, second, by the nature of the external circumstances, the mothering, in which that drive finds opportunity for satisfaction.

There is also a third determinant of the ultimate quality of

---

[3] See this process discussed in Hans Loewald, "On the Therapeutic Action of Psychoanalysis," *International Journal of Psychoanalysis*, XLI (1960), 24.

these new functions and subjective experiences, for the fact is that such results are not the same for all babies and would not be so even with identical patterns of mothering. The additional determinant is the initial configuration of tension-organizing forms. Thus, the drive impetus is experienced in the first place according to the dimensions and qualities of subjective experience imposed by such factors as tension thresholds, degree of sucking readiness—according to which some babies seem to experience tension in a more directed form (as sucking tension), whereas others give evidence of a more diffuse tension experience—and the like.

To these factors that determine the initial tension experience, one must add many more that influence the quality of all the functions that are engaged in the mothering process. There are differences in anticipation capacity enabling one baby to develop expectant (and trusting) directedness of tension more quickly than another, differences in motor coordination, general differences in bodily sensation that seem to make one baby need to be rocked while nursing and another not or seem to make one more interested in being cuddled than another, and so on. All these factors that determine or reflect the baby's initial mode of tension organization and way of functioning, not even to mention factors that specifically influence the baby's perception of the mother, determine differences in the extent and direction of development not only of the quality of the experience of the drive tension itself, but also of the various functions that develop under the impetus of the drive tension. It is from this initial style, if one may speak of it this early, that the subjective form of the drive and the specific shape of the psychological capacities associated with it are crystallized by mothering.

This process could be described in essentially the same way for later stages of drive development and later stages of maturation in general. Later, in fact, when the existing style of functioning is more clearly defined, it is even more apparent that its further development under the impact of fresh drives depends not only on the nature of those drives or the nature of external circumstances, but also on its own nature, its own susceptibilities for development, that is, its development under such impact consists of special differentiations of general style tendencies. Thus, one may imagine a precociously intense, alert, and active little boy becoming obstinate under a regime that attempts to deprive him of the satisfying experience of exercising his own bowel control or other willful and volitional functions, whereas a passive and babyish youngster, at the same time and under the same regime, becomes not merely passive, but, more specifically, submissive.

In any particular instance, whatever the details of the interplay between the style-modifying tendencies of a given stage of instinctual drive and maturation, on the one hand, and the existing style, on the other, the outcome can only be reconciliation and mutual change. The press of an instinctual drive, with its own potentialities for new kinds of subjective experience, behavior, and the like, and the fresh developmental equipment and tendency associated with it further differentiate the general style of functioning in one direction or another, whereas these drives and new developmental tendencies are ultimately organized by that general style. The shape of their subjective experience, their degree of modulation, the general form of their behavioral manifestations, and so forth are finally consistent with what is generally characteristic of the individual.

The Control and Regulative Function of Styles

After an initial period of predominant interest in the nature and development of instinctual drives, psychoanalytic attention turned increasingly toward problems of how drive tensions, pressing for immediate discharge and satisfaction, are restrained and subjected to controls and how and by what means tension is maintained and modulated and the individual thereby stabi·

lized. That is, attention turned to the domain of the "ego." The primary importance of this interest was clinical, for, in neurotic conditions, drive-tension restraints break down or fail to develop, with resulting discomfort, necessity for extraordinary countermeasures, and symptom formation.

But the capacity for restraint or delay of tension discharge has far more general significance as well. The development of thinking and the replacement of immediate discharge into action by reflection and the imagining of action, the development and refinement of affects, the development of all the "higher" functions and the modulation of all the basic ones, and, in general, the individual's transformation from a condition of relative helplessness vis-à-vis peremptory tensions to a condition of smooth discharge, of intentionality, and of "will"—all of these depend on, among other factors, an increasingly refined capacity for tension maintenance and control. But this does not mean "control" in the ordinary, common-sense meaning of the term. It does not mean control on the part of the individual or "will power," but control of an automatic kind on the part of the ego, a department of the individual.

I have attributed to psychological styles or the structures that they reflect an organizing and stabilizing function. I have described these structures as contributing to the continuity and stability of the individual and, in effect, as tension regulators. The question arises, therefore, of the position and function of styles in the development of these drive-tension controls.

Psychoanalysis originally conceived of such controls as counterforces opposing and restraining instinctual tensions but came later to a concept of structures, for example, defenses, in which such restraints were more or less stably consolidated. Initially, these restraining counterforces or structures were thought to arise entirely under the impact of instinct-prohibiting, satisfaction-denying, or delaying external realities. Later considerations—once again, the fact of innate psychological apparatuses—prompted an amendment of this view. Even the existence of minimal innate apparatuses implies some degree of innate tension-maintaining psychological structure. Thus, even the existence of tension-discharge thresholds—for example, thresholds for the setting into operation of motility apparatuses—that establish a level below which tension will be maintained may be regarded, it has been thought, as innate nuclei around which more elaborate tension-maintaining or control structures may later develop.[4]

This concept of innate nuclei of tension-maintaining or control structures reminds us once again that the image of infantile helplessness or passivity vis-à-vis drive tension, that is, the image of immediate tension discharge, is only a picture of a theoretical extreme, a model based on an extrapolation of a tendency. In actual fact, it is clearly impossible for any psychological state (or biological one) to be devoid of tension-maintaining or control structures. Here, in fact, we may again ask the question whether this picture of innate tension maintenance elements, in such a skeletal form as that of tension thresholds, does full justice to the significance of those innate apparatuses.

I have suggested that the picture of an assemblage of innate apparatuses may be extrapolated somewhat to a picture of an initial organizing configuration, a configuration of innate equipment that imposes a primitive organization on the infant's experience and discharge of drive tensions (as well as experience of and response to external stimulation). Now I would like to consider the further proposition that this same initial organizing configuration, the first rough determinant of individual style, may also be regarded as an initial tension-maintaining or control structure not only in its threshold aspects, but also in its organizing aspects. Let me clarify this.

Generally speaking, control may exist in the form of a specific counterforce or restraining structure or it may be an aspect, a component vector, so to speak, of an organization of energy that

---

[4] David Rapaport emphasized this point. See David Rapaport, "The Conceptual Model of Psychoanalysis," *Journal of Personality*, 20 (1951), 56–81.

accomplishes other results as well. The main aim and design of a dam, for example, is the production of electric power, but the transformation of energy involved in this production necessarily entails an aspect of restraint of the original force. Indeed, restraint and transformation of energy are in this sense necessarily linked; no restraint of continuously supplied energy is possible without transformation, and no transformation is possible without a component of restraint.

The infant comes equipped for certain modes of experiencing and discharging, that is, organizing, tension however primitive these may as yet be. For instance, he comes equipped to suck, with a psychological "readiness" for sucking, and a "readiness" to respond to the nipple. If this innate "readiness" is well established and if it is adequately coordinated with certain physical capacities and apparatuses, then what would otherwise be discharged in diffuse activity tends instead to be manifested in sucking, and what would otherwise be experienced as a less differentiated tension is experienced in a more differentiated and directed form.

To the extent that this occurs, one may speak of this "readiness," that is, the total psychological equipment that allows for a more differentiated mode of experience and discharge, as a tension-organizing and tension-maintaining structure. One may imagine, in other words, that the infant who is better equipped in this way has a relatively higher threshold for tension discharge in diffuse activity, is able to "tolerate" more. At this point, however, it is necessary to consider the further development of tension-maintaining capacity in order to make the relationship between it and psychological organizing structures clearer.

Let us remember the process I described earlier in which originally less differentiated urges of a baby achieve increased organization and direction. In the course of experience, an initially less differentiated tension finds an external object, and, gradually, the baby comes not only to anticipate or expect satisfaction, but also to experience the tension in a more directed way and ultimately to learn to cry *for* the mother. This means that new tension-organizing equipment has been developed. What has happened to the original tension with the development of this new organizing equipment? It has disappeared in its previous form. Where there was relatively diffuse tension, there is now directed, expectant activity. To the extent that such new organizing equipment is created, tension is converted into *intention; a tension-maintaining structure has been created and it is not different from the organizing structure itself.*

To summarize, when psychological organizing equipment is advanced and modes of functioning further developed and differentiated, the individual's condition is advanced from one of relative helplessness vis-à-vis drive tensions to one of greater intentionality, and relatively diffuse tension is converted into intentional, directed activity and expectation. One aspect of this process may be described as the development of tension-maintaining capacity or capacity to restrain, postpone, or control discharge. This increased capacity for control or restraint of tension discharge occurs not because of any infantile will power, but because the form of tension has been changed; the existence of anticipations, expectations, and directedness has, so to speak, revised the meaning of control or restraint. To the extent that tension is undifferentiated—lacking in subjective organization, aim, or direction—it seems to be essentially unrestrainable, and, to that extent, immediate discharge in one form or another takes place. On the other hand, to the extent that tension has been converted to or exists in the form of intention, anticipation, and directed activity, it does not require further restraint but will, within certain limits, automatically be maintained. From this point of view, increased organization of tension, increased intentionality, and increased capacity for tension discharge delay are all aspects of the same process.[5]

---

[5] I am not able to say what the relationship of this process may be to the process described as "binding." Possibly, they are identical. See Robert R. Holt, "A Critical Examination of Freud's Concept of Bound versus Free

Style and Defense

The relationship between style and defense may be described simply. The individual's style of functioning—of thinking, for instance—characterizes defensive operations as well as all others and determines their particular shape. Approximately the same formulation is expressed by Holzman. "The style of defense may be dictated by the general life style of the person, as developed from the constitutional, maturational, and experiential vec-

---

Cathexis," *Journal of the American Psychoanalytic Association*, X, No. 3 (July 1962), 475–525.

It may be that, within certain limits, a parallel process can be described in connection with perceptual development. In other words, the development of perception from a condition of relative passivity vis-à-vis external stimuli, for example, distractability by what is sensorially compelling, to a condition of intentional, mobile attention may be described as a development of perceptual organizing equipment and, with this, more advanced perceptual and cognitive modes. Senden's description of congenitally blind people learning form vision after initially being dazzled by colors, shininess, and the like seems to support this view; see M. von Senden, *Notes on "Raum-und Gestaltaufassung bei Operierten Blindgeborenen vor und nach der Operation"* [1932], trans. (Cornell University: Laboratory of Psychology, June 1950), mimeographed. See also David Shapiro, "A Perceptual Understanding of Color-Response," *Rorschach Psychology*, ed. by M. Rickers-Ovsiankina (New York: Wiley, 1960), pp. 154–201. It is also possible to understand the innate "stimulus barrier," suggested by Freud, along these lines. That is, the stimulus barrier need not be regarded as merely a protective shield against excessive stimuli, a conception that would seem more in tune with a passive model of perception and would hardly distinguish the psychological stimulus barrier from what could be accomplished by anatomical protective devices. Instead, the psychological stimulus barrier may be regarded as an aspect or result of innate perceptual organizing capacity, the greater the innate organizing equipment, the less susceptibility to undifferentiated, compelling sensory stimuli. The absolute capacity of the infant for perceptual organization is, of course, limited, but individual differences may still be significant. It seems to me, although I am not certain of this, that Dr. Sibylle Escalona also suggested such a point of view in a lecture at the Austen Riggs Center some years ago.

tors." [6] Another formulation, but one that seems to me less satisfactory, states that the defensive process "makes use of" modes of thought that are generally characteristic of the individual.[7]

All of these formulations are satisfactory in a general way, but they are still highly schematic, and, in fact, they contain certain unclarities that may not be immediately apparent. The problem is this. Defenses may be regarded as tension-controlling or regulative structures, and, as I have suggested, styles may likewise be regarded as reflecting regulative structures. Are we then to imagine regulators "making use of" regulators? [8] It is best, at any rate, to state more concretely and to illustrate what I mean by saying that the defensive functioning of an individual is characterized by his general style of functioning. I will do this first by describing, as carefully as I can, defensive functioning in process, that is, in a condition of relative instability.

When an affect, drive tension, or derivative, accompanied by excessive discomfort or anxiety, is or threatens to be experienced consciously, that experience is of such a sort as to move the individual, according to his style, to some tension-reducing function. He is moved to some feeling, thought, and often action, one result of which, although not the only one, being the elimination from consciousness of the incipient experience and its attendant discomfort.

Before we consider an illustration, let me call attention to two features of this view of the defensive process. First, the process is one in which the conscious individual actively participates,

---

[6] Philip S. Holzman, "Repression and Cognitive Style," *Bulletin of the Menninger Clinic* XXVI, No. 6 (November, 1962), 277.

[7] *Ibid.*, p. 281.

[8] These definitions are further complicated, unless I am mistaken, by an ambiguity of language to which I also plead guilty. Psychological writers have a tendency to use "style" in two ways. One is descriptive of a formal consistency, presumably resulting from form-giving structures. Another use, however, casts style *as* a form-giving structure. The latter use, however, happens to be quite convenient.

not by choice, but simply by being what he is. This is in contrast to the "marionette" viewpoint that regards him as passively protected by defenses from threatening or discomforting tensions. Second, since the process is one in which the particular and characteristic experience of a special tension automatically triggers some characteristic tension-reducing function, it is a process by which a psychological state is self-stabilizing and self-maintaining. This view, in other words, follows those, particularly Menninger,[9] who have argued for a "homeostatic" understanding of defensive processes. Now let me illustrate.

An obsessive-compulsive patient—a sober, technically minded, and active man—was usually conspicuously lacking in enthusiasm or excitement in circumstances that might seem to warrant them. On one occasion, as he talked about a certain prospect of his, namely, the good chance of an important success in his work, his sober expression was momentarily interrupted by a smile. After a few more minutes of talking, during which he maintained his soberness only with difficulty, he began quite hesitantly to speak of certain hopes that he had only alluded to earlier. Then he broke into a grin. Almost immediately, however, he regained his usual, somewhat worried expression. As he did this, he said, "Of course, the outcome is by no means certain," and he said this in a tone that, if anything, would suggest that the outcome was almost certain to be a failure. After ticking off several of the specific possibilities for a hitch, he finally seemed to be himself again, so to speak.

This man experienced or began to experience an affect and an idea that made him visibly uncomfortable. A defensive process operated in such a way as to block or at least reduce the intensity of that affect and idea, and he regained his comfort. Let us attempt to reconstruct some aspects of that process.

The experience as well as the actual expression of slight enthusiasm may seem a trivial matter from a normal point of view but not from this man's standpoint. He had often expressed his

---

[9] Karl Menninger (with Martin Mayman and Paul Pruyser), *The Vital Balance* (New York: The Viking Press, 1963).

views about "premature" hopes or enthusiasm. To dwell on such hopes was childish and unrealistic. While he did not believe that the mere expression or feeling of enthusiasm would diminish the chances of success in any magical way, in another, quasilogical way, he felt that it might. For enthusiasm, according to his lights, could lead one into a "fool's paradise" and thence to careless or reckless behavior.

These views and this fancy reasoning cannot, themselves, be held responsible for blocking the incipient affect, since, no matter what his preference might be, he was no more capable of personal thought control than the next person. But the nature of these views does reflect the quality of discomforting experience that this particular affect entails for him, that is, the quality of his personal translation of the incipient affect. It *felt* reckless to him. This man, on occasions in the past when feeling some unusual affect or when tempted to some piece of spontaneous behavior, had experienced with considerable anxiety the feeling that he might "go crazy," "lose control," or the like, and it is safe to say that, on this occasion, he experienced something of the kind in modified or diminished form. What he experienced, in other words, is strictly speaking and according to his subjective definition not enthusiasm at all, even though it started out to be enthusiasm. His experience was or rapidly became a different, probably less modulated one of excitement, perhaps temptation to recklessness, and apprehension.

The careful man, when he feels in danger of recklessly overestimating his position, takes precautions. He did not decide to become a careful man; he simply is one. He examines his prospects for flaws or imperfections and easily finds some. These are not imagined flaws, but actual if somewhat remote ones. They are the products of the sharp, searching attention to which he has already been moved by his nervousness. These flaws, the flies in the ointment, now dominate his awareness, and, characteristically, he loses a sense of their proportion to the whole picture. When this occurs, any incipient enthusiasm or excitement as well as any discomfort associated with those affects—the feeling of recklessness, in other words—disappears from consciousness or at least is appreciably reduced in awareness. He no longer needs to struggle not to grin; he is not in a grinning mood. He does not will this process, and he cannot will it away, but he, and not only a department of him, is very much a part of it.

How shall we describe this particular defensive process? It is nothing else than the automatic operation of the obsessive-compulsive style of functioning itself. A discomforting affect, inconsistent with and intolerable to the existing style, is experienced according to the viewpoint of that style, that is, as recklessness, and automatically moves the individual to thoughts and behavior that reduce the tension and lead to a more characteristic frame of mind in which the original affect and its discomfort disappear. A state of tension has been organized according to the prevailing style and has led to a characteristic tension-reducing function.

The defensive process described may, therefore, be regarded as a special case of the operation of the general style of functioning, namely, the operation of that style under special conditions of tension. Insofar as any style represents a tension-organizing system, it may be said to have self-maintaining aspects, that is, the capacity to organize unusual tensions in familiar ways; under conditions of special tension, these self-maintaining aspects become especially visible. Thus, the obsessive-compulsive person, tempted to an unusual enthusiasm, feels the necessity to look for a fly in the ointment. The paranoid person, momentarily inclined to a less guarded action, discovers a suspicious clue in the nick of time. The hysterical woman who begins to assert a sharply defined position suddenly becomes aware of the insufficiency of her qualifications and, in a rush of embarrassment, forgets what she had to say altogether. The impulsive person who plays with the idea of a serious, long-range plan feels uncomfortably burdened, and, to him, the only next thing to do is to get a drink.

We may describe these unusual tensions in terms of their counterparts in normal experience, but, to the neurotic person, they are not equivalent to the normal experience. To the paranoid person, an unguarded action is very serious business because he feels vulnerable, and, for someone who feels vulnerable, what is there to do but to check once more? In each case, in other words, a state of tension is created that can only be experienced according to the modes of function in existence and can only move the individual in some direction that will diminish it. Of course, such a process does not eliminate the underlying sources of the particular tension, but only prevents conscious development of it.

The difference between the defensive process under special conditions of tension or in a condition of transient instability and more stable defensive functioning is essentially a difference in degree. Defensive functioning is an aspect and a continuous one of all neurotic functioning insofar as any neurotic style tends to inhibit the development into consciousness of tendencies that diverge from it. Under certain conditions, a neurotic mode of functioning may operate with sufficient smoothness as to prevent all but negligible amounts of special tension from arising. In such people, sometimes called "well-integrated" neurotics, one will not necessarily see the apparently exaggerated forms of neurotic functioning that give evidence of the style operating under conditions of special tension or instability.

Certain corollaries follow from this view of defense. I shall mention three.

(1) The defensive process cannot be regarded merely as an operation of specific drive-inhibiting mechanisms, since it involves the whole drive-tension and stimulus-organizing style. On the contrary, if this viewpoint is correct, the commonly listed defense mechanisms should be susceptible to analysis in terms of the thought and attention processes, affect modes, and the like, that are involved in them—analysis, in other words, as aspects or features of more general modes of functioning.

(2) Any defensive process, insofar as it is an aspect of the organization of tension according to certain forms, excludes from consciousness not merely specific mental contents, but *classes* of mental content and subjective experience. Thus, in a compulsive person, not only may certain aggressive impulses and their derivatives or certain passive impulses and their derivatives be excluded from consciousness, but also whole classes of affects, cognitions, and of motivational experiences. It may be noted that this fact has a certain implication for psychotherapy, namely, that the defensive process may be confronted therapeutically over a very great range of psychological content, including the apparently "superficial."

(3) The defensive process is not, strictly speaking, an entirely intrapsychic process. Since it involves the whole style of functioning, it involves, at several points, the individual's relationship to external reality. Thus, the neurotic person's mode of activity, including his characteristic mode of communication as well as his mode of apprehension of the external world, are all likely, at various times, to be essential elements of defensive functioning.

The Defensive Motives for Neurotic Styles

If we say that a consequence of any neurotic style is the exclusion from consciousness of certain classes of subjective experience and mental content, can we say further that such an exclusion, a defensive measure, in other words, was the reason or motive for the neurotic style in the first place?

It is clear that, among the "reasons" for or causes of any style, neurotic or otherwise, there are many factors that are not motivational at all. I refer not only to the innate and maturational factors, but also to a great many environmental factors—physical, social, and cultural—that make up the climate in which innate potentialities develop. These are facts of history that certainly influence the ultimate nature of psychological style but that do not involve motives or instinctual conflict. The existence of such sources, independent of instinctual conflict, means that the nature of a style can never be attributed simply to such dynamic factors as defensive requirements. On the other hand, these nonmotivational sources of style cannot by themselves be held responsible for the development of neurosis and the crystallization of neurotic styles from more general forms. They cannot be held accountable, in other words, for the continuous, uncomfortable attenuation, distortion, or elimination from consciousness of tendencies and inclinations to new kinds of experience and function that is a part of every neurotic style.

When a relatively stable, adult neurotic style is subject to an intolerable tension, we may expect a defensive intensification of function that eliminates the tension. The adult's ways of moving under the impetus of such tensions are relatively cut and dried. But what happens in comparable circumstances in childhood? What happens, in other words, when a child is subject to an unusual tension—let us say, a fresh drive tension for which no satisfactory mode or organizing form is as yet established and, let us say further, for which external and / or internal conditions are such as to prevent any such form from being established, that is, differentiated from existing forms?

The answer in most cases is obvious. If a mode cannot be achieved that organizes the existing drive tension in a modulated, smoothly dischargeable form and permits the development of the affective potentialities, activity capacities, and the like, coordinated with that tension, then a mode will develop that eliminates the tension by other means. A new differentiation of organizing forms appears that is capable of restoring stability in exactly the way in which an adult neurotic style functions defensively, namely, by eliminating the tension or aspects of it from consciousness. Thus, the given drive tension, discomforting and intolerable, moves the child, in accordance with his style and in accordance with the particular way in which he experiences that discomfort, to feelings, thoughts, or activity that tend to reduce that tension. New affects, kinds of thinking, and behavior develop, but they do not realize the full potentialities of the developmental stage. Thus, instead of a new experience of pride and an interest in exercising new volitional capacities, there may be new rigidity and shame; instead of initiative leading to new interests, there may be inhibition; and so on. A new but neurotic differentiation will have arisen from the general style of functioning, and comparative stability will have been restored in a direction that restricts and distorts not only drives, but also ego development.

Such neurotic differentiations have an interesting sidelight. On the one hand, insofar as they cramp the normal, full development of cognition, affect, and activity and tend to become increasingly stable and self-maintaining, they lead up a blind alley. On the other hand, insofar as they accomplish defensive ends by the development of special distortions of function, they very often lead to hypertrophy—as compared with the normal— of certain capacities with specific adaptive advantages. Thus, the impulsive person may have excellent practical know-how, the psychopath may have highly developed social charm, the paranoid person may have acuteness of observation, the obsessive-compulsive may have a prodigious capacity for work, and so on.

We may conclude, then, that defensive requirements certainly influence the course of style development. But it is far from correct to imagine, as Reich did, that, under given drive conditions, the resultant character directly reflects the specific nature of the external prohibition. On the contrary, the outcome, the neurotic differentiation, is quite different given different pre-existing modes of functioning. It is to this fact, incidentally, that we may attribute the clinical commonplace that dynamic explanation may be entirely sound retrospectively and yet provide us with little predictive advantage. It is in the nature of the subject matter that the same circumstances of drive and external reality produce a number of different outcomes, and we may, therefore, hope for only partial correlations between such circumstances and ultimate psychological condition.

Index

Abraham, Karl, 6

action, impulsive, 139–147

activity, "driven" character of, 33; in neurotic functioning, 18; of obsessive-compulsive person, 30–48

Adler, Alfred, 17 n.

adolescence, concentration in, 29

adult styles, innate determination of, 180–181

affect, drive tension and, 182–185; isolation of, 108; "explosions" of, 124–128; hysterical, 128–131; moral values and, 159; restriction of in obsessive-compulsive, 43–44; restriction of in paranoid, 77; "shallow," 129, 132, 142

alcoholics, 21–22, 134–135, 169–170

amnesia, 70

anal-erotic impulses, 5

arrogance, in paranoiac person, 81, 85

attention, biased, 59; directedness of, 58–59; fuzzing of, 59; mobility of, 27–30; in obsessive-compulsive person, 27; in paranoid person, 58–59; see also cognition

authority, paranoid person's resentment of, 84

autism, 66; projection and, 70

autonomy, in children, 35; competency and, 81–82; experience of, 30–48; homosexuality and, 86; hypertrophy of functions of, 80;

obsessive-compulsive versus paranoid, 107; obsessive-compulsive's activity mode and, 30 ff; in paranoid person, 73–104; see also volition; will

bias, in paranoid person, 61; projection and, 73

bodily sensation, in paranoid style, 78; tension development and, 178

body musculature, in paranoid person, 73–74

boss, resentment of in paranoid person, 60, 72, 85, 89, 96, 102

character, defined, 5; early psychoanalytic papers on, 6; hardening of, 8; infantile instinctual conflict and, 7–8; psychoanalytic psychology of, 4–15; specific form of symptom as problem of, 5; as total formation, 7; understanding of, 4

character traits, origin of, 6, 14

childhood and children, autonomy in, 35; behavior and, 21; cognition of, 29; drive tensions in, 197–198; intentionality in, 82; negativism in, 82; stubbornness in, 82; volitional behavior in, 35, 82; willfulness in, 82; see also infant

choice, of neurosis, 4, 10, 17; in passive-submissive person, 170–174; see also decision-making